Read! Perform! Learn! 2

10 Reader's Theater Programs
for Literacy Enhancement

Toni Buzzeo

UpstartBooks

Fort Atkinson, Wisconsin

With thanks to my friend and art director, Heidi Green,
who brings all of my graphic ideas to life on the page.

Reader's Theater Permissions:

Page 10: Adapted from *Axle Annie and the Speed Grump* by Robin Pulver, © 2005 by Robin Pulver, text. Used by permission of Dial Books for Young Readers, A Member of Penguin Group (USA) Inc. All rights reserved.

Page 24: Adapted from *Bee-bim Bop!* by Linda Sue Park. Text © 2005 by Linda Sue Park. Adapted and reprinted by permission of Clarion Books, an imprint of Houghton Mifflin Company. All rights reserved.

Page 37: *The Boy Who Drew Birds: A Story of John James Audubon* by Jacqueline Davies. Text © 2004 by Jacqueline Davies. Adapted and reprinted by permission of Houghton Mifflin Company. All rights reserved.

Page 56: *Button, Bucket, Sky* by Jacqueline Briggs Martin; illustrated by Vicki Jo Redenbaugh. Text © 1998 by Jacqueline Briggs Martin. Illustrations © 1998 by Vicki Jo Redenbaugh. Use of illustrations and the creation and publication of a dramatic adaptation of this work made possible through permission of Carolrhoda Books, a division of Lerner Publishing Group, Inc. All rights reserved.

Page 70: Adapted from *Even Firefighters Hug Their Moms* by Christine Kole MacLean, illustrated by Mike Reed, © 2002 by Christine Kole MacLean, text. Used by permission of Dutton Children's Books, a Division of Penguin Young Readers Group, a Member of Penguin Group (USA) Inc. All rights reserved.

Page 84: *Faraway Home,* text © 2000 by Jane Kurtz, adapted and reprinted by permission of Harcourt, Inc.

Page 99: From *Freedom Summer* by Deborah Wiles. Text © 2001 by Deborah Wiles. Reprinted with permission of Atheneum Books for Young Readers, an imprint of Simon & Schuster Children's Publishing Division. All rights reserved.

Page 111: Text and jacket design from *Monsoon* by Uma Krishnaswami, illustrated by Jaime Akib. Text © 2003 by Uma Krishnaswami. Pictures © 2003 by Jaime Akib. Reprinted by permission of Farrar, Straus and Giroux, LLC.

Page 121: *My Brother's Flying Machine* by Jane Yolen. Used by permission of Curtis Brown, Ltd. © 2003. All rights reserved.

Page 141: *Oliver's Must-Do List* by Susan Taylor Brown, illustrated by Mary Sullivan. Reprinted with the permission of Boyds Mills Perss, Inc. Text © 2005 by Susan Taylor Brown; illustrations © 2005 by Mary Sullivan.

Published by UpstartBooks
W5527 State Road 106
P.O. Box 800
Fort Atkinson, Wisconsin 53538-0800
1-800-448-4887

The paper used in this publication meets the minimum requirements of American National Standard for Information Science — Permanence of Paper for Printed Library Material. ANSI/NISO Z39.48-1992.

Contents

Introduction

Reader's theater is an exciting way to share literature with children and provide them with an opportunity to enjoy meaningful participation and effective reading practice simultaneously. What's more, reader's theater is a LOT of fun!

According to a study conducted by Dr. Carol Corcoran and A. Dia Davis published in *Reading Improvement* [1], "Reader's theater is effective in improving student interest in reading, confidence in reading, and overall fluency in number of words read correctly per minute." It's really no wonder. Unlike the pressure of round robin reading where students might be expected to read aloud from unfamiliar text, reader's theater offers readers the opportunity to become familiar in advance with the text they will read, to practice it until they are fluent with it, and then to relish the positive experience of reading that well-practiced text aloud for an audience.

In a *Reading Teacher* article entitled "I Thought about It All Night," [2] Jo Worthy and Kathryn Prater tout the advantages of reader's theater for even challenged readers, noting that it "combines several effective research-based practices, but also leads to increased engagement with literacy even in very resistant readers." Worthy and Prater emphasize that with regular reading performances, "all students have the opportunity to practice, successfully perform, and increase their self-confidence." Those are three worthy goals!

Read! Perform! Learn! Volume 2, 10 Reader's Theater Programs for Literacy Enhancement is a resource for school library media specialists, public children's librarians, and classroom teachers who want to share excellent children's literature with their students while improving reading skills and extending the use of books into the content areas, meeting learning standards in English Language Arts and beyond.

How to Use This Book

Contents

In this book, you will find ten chapters, each devoted to one picture book. For each book, you will find an author interview, a reader's theater script, and a set of standards-based learning activities with accompanying standards.

Preparation

Begin by reading the children's book you have chosen and the author interview yourself to become familiar with the story and its creator. Next, read the book aloud to students so that they can enjoy the illustrations and appreciate the nuances of the story as revealed through the art. Students will carry these visual images into their reader's theater experience. Finally, share the interview with students either by reading the questions and responses aloud to them (for older students) or by paraphrasing and sharing the information with younger students.

Using the Reader's Theater Script

Once you have read the script and matched students with parts—paying special attention to the level of challenge each part will pose for your various student readers—distribute a set of photocopied scripts to the readers. Ask the remaining children to be the audience. Allow readers to practice, providing as much support and advice as necessary to allow each child to deliver a successful reading.

Invite performers to face the audience and simply read their parts in turn on the first full-cast run-through. Once all of the readers are comfortable with their parts, you are ready to stage a second reading with the opportunity to use props or costumes, if desired. Suggestions for each are provided in the introductory material for the script. You may also invite students to act out the story while reading.

Extending the Learning

Because literature can be a meaningful introduction to classroom or collaborative content area units or provide an extension of units under study, each script is accompanied by a set of standards-based learning activities for each of the ten featured books to accompany and extend student learning. Individual content area standards are drawn from the McREL document Content Knowledge: A Compendium of Standards and Benchmarks for K–12 Education, 4th Edition available at www.mcrel.org/standards-benchmarks/. In addition to English Language Arts activities, you will find activities for Science, Social Studies, Math, Art, Music, Physical Education, and Life Skills. I hope that these activities will help deepen your students' experience of the books while meeting content standards in several disciplines.

Most of all, however, I hope that you enjoy the books I have chosen, their talented authors, and the fun of sharing them through reader's theater with your students!

A Note about Web sites: Because Web sites are constantly evolving, if you find a URL listed here that is no longer active, you might try performing a keyword search on the Web site title or domain name to locate the new URL.

---

1. Carol A. Corcoran and A. Dia Davis, "A Study of the Effects of Readers' Theater on Second and Third Grade Special Education Students' Fluency Growth," *Reading Improvement* 42, no. 2 (Summer 2005):105–111.

2. Jo Worthy and Kathryn Prater, "'I thought about it all night': Readers Theatre for Reading Fluency and Motivation," *Reading Teacher* 56, no. 3 (November 2002): 294–297.

Axle Annie and the Speed Grump

Read *Axle Annie and the Speed Grump* and the interview with Robin Pulver below to familiarize yourself with the book and the author. Read the book aloud to children first, so that they can enjoy the illustrations and become familiar with the story. Then, hand out a set of photocopied scripts to thirteen students. Ask the remaining children to be the audience (or if your class is relatively small, make the chorus bigger and involve them all). Have performers face the audience and simply read their parts on the first run-through. Once all readers are comfortable with their parts, have a second reading with the opportunity to use props or costumes if desired, and to act out the story while reading.

Meet Robin Pulver

Robin grew up in upstate New York and lived in Oregon, Idaho, Ohio, and Zambia (East Africa) with her husband Don, before settling in Pittsford, New York, to raise a family. Her early writing was journalism and adult fiction. Then, reading aloud with her children, Nina and David, inspired her to write for children. When not visiting schools or writing, Robin enjoys playing with her bouncy labradoodle (Sadie), hiking, bird-watching, cross-country skiing, swimming, reading, theater, movies, and meeting with her writers' groups. In addition to the Axle Annie books, other Robin Pulver books include *Author Day for Room 3T, Punctuation Takes a Vacation, Christmas for a Kitten, Nouns and Verbs Have a Field Day,* and the popular Mrs. Toggle series.

Where did the character of Axle Annie come from? She seems so familiar a school character (as did your much-beloved teacher and the wide cast of characters in the Mrs. Toggle books). It's amazing you haven't been a teacher!

RP: I'd been wanting to write a school bus driver story for some time. A picture of rock star Axl Rose on the cover of *Spin* magazine inspired me. Often, it's finding the right name that helps me through the process of bringing a character to life. Axle Rose (note the added e) seemed like a great name for a woman school bus driver! I called my char-

acter Axle Rose, then Rose Axle, then Axle Rosie as I wrote draft after draft after draft. Finally, she became Axle Annie. Of course I needed to give the main character a problem. Winter driving **can** be a problem for me. I decided to write a story about a character who is much braver about driving in the snow than I am. That was a challenge I gave myself. And then I gave Axle Annie the much bigger challenge of driving up Tiger Hill in snowstorms! That was the first book, *Axle Annie*.

By the way, I admire teachers and owe a lot to them, but I never considered becoming a schoolteacher, because I was always terrified of speaking in front of people. Funny, isn't it, that now, because of my writing, I find myself driving (often in snow) to schools to speak in front of people!

Readers who read your earlier book, *Axle Annie*, are familiar with the lovable, optimistic, and determined bus driver. Does she plan to have more adventures beyond *Axle Annie and the Speed Grump*? If so, can you speculate what else might happen?

RP: I love Axle Annie. I love sharing her stories with kids. Part of the reason I love her so much is Tedd Arnold's brilliant illustrations, which certainly bring her to life. I'm not sure whether there will be other adventures, though. I sold *Axle Annie and the Speed Grump* **six years** before it was published! Tedd, who is a successful author as well as illustrator, was so booked up with projects it was a few years before he could tackle the illustrations. Meanwhile, I haven't written another Axle Annie. Of course I have thought about other adventures. Maybe I would write about a bully on the bus, or a challenging field trip, or a bus maintenance problem, or some other problem

that all school bus drivers find themselves contending with. I'm open to suggestions!

Many adults assume that children's writers begin a story with a lesson in mind they want to teach their young readers. That, of course, isn't often true. But *Axle Annie and the Speed Grump* is a story with a strong message about the consequences of being unmannerly as well as ignoring rules and laws. Did you have that lesson in mind when you began?

RP: I wouldn't say that I had a lesson in mind. I usually start a story with a problem and then find a main character to go with it. But in both of the Axle Annie books, I started with the main character. Then I needed to find a problem for her, one that readers could identify with. A universal problem for school bus drivers is reckless, thoughtless drivers like Rush Hotfoot. For Rush Hotfoot, the consequences came naturally as I wrote the story.

You invented the Grouch and Grump Club in your first Annie book, *Axle Annie*. What role do you feel the club plays in helping you tell the Annie stories?

RP: The Grouch and Grump Club adds humor and change of pace. It gives the characters a chance to talk out their problems in dialogue. It was also my way, as the author, of offering the illustrator a break from being on the school bus. In picture books, it's important for authors to provide changes of scene for illustrators to work with. I thought it would be fun to bring in some kind of club, because I think kids like the idea of clubs. I know I did.

So—when writing *Axle Annie and the Speed Grump*—I wanted to give the story the

same shape as *Axle Annie*. The Grouch and Grump Club brings Axle Annie and Rush Hotfoot face to face in this story.

You must have had many conversations with young readers about Rush Hotfoot and his behavior throughout the story. How have these readers felt about Axle Annie's response when Rush is in trouble? How have they responded to Annie's caring for her fellow human being, despite his rudeness?

RP: This is a fascinating question. Most kids don't question Annie's caring, at least not to me. But one did recently ask, "Why did Annie help Rush if he's so bad?" I expect he was voicing a question in other young readers' minds. I suppose this gets to the root of my personal value system. I believe in forgiveness and second chances, and that belief creeps into my stories. Some people, like Rush Hotfoot, just need to learn hard lessons. That said, I wanted to be very, very careful in this story that Annie didn't risk her own, or her kids' safety, when she rescued Rush Hotfoot. So I consulted with a number of bus drivers about what she could do.

Upstate New York, where you grew up and now live is an enormously snowy place in the winter. Do you have interesting snow stories to tell from your life?

RP: Oh, sure! Until I was seven, my family lived in a small country house at the top of a big hill. One storm blew the snow in drifts up to our second story window. We were stuck in our house. We couldn't get out the door. In those years, I rode a bus to my school, which was at the top of another huge hill, Tiger Hill in Phelps, New York.

The town used to close Tiger Hill to traffic in the winter, so we kids could use it for sledding. Very exciting and scary!

How can readers learn more about you and your books?

RP: Please visit my Web site at www.robinpulver.com. You'll find a bio, information about my books and school visits, a Q & A for writers, and bookmarks and coloring sheets to print out.

Books by Robin Pulver

Alicia's Tutu. Dial, 1997.

Author Day for Room 3T. Clarion, 2005.

Axle Annie. Dial, 2002.

Axle Annie and the Speed Grump. Dial, 2005.

Christmas for a Kitten. Albert Whitman, 2003.

The Holiday Handwriting School. Simon & Schuster, 1991.

Homer and the House Next Door. Simon & Schuster, 1994.

Mrs. Toggle's Beautiful Blue Shoe. Simon & Schuster, 1994.

Mrs. Toggle's Class Picture Day. Scholastic, 2000.

Mrs. Toggle and the Dinosaur. Simon & Schuster, 1991.

Mrs. Toggle's Zipper. Simon & Schuster, 1990.

Nobody's Mother Is in Second Grade. Dial, 1992.

Nouns and Verbs Have a Field Day. Holiday House, 2006.

Punctuation Takes a Vacation. Holiday House, 2003.

Way To Go, Alex! Albert Whitman, 1999.

Axle Annie and the Speed Grump Script

Roles

Axle Annie	Rush Hotfoot	Kids (Five readers)
Narrator One	Narrator Two	Narrator Three
Chorus (Three readers)		

Narrator One: Axle Annie was the best school bus driver in Burskyville. She loved the kids, and the kids loved her.

Narrator Two: Riding on her bus was one of their favorite parts of the day.

Narrator Three: But Annie and the kids had a problem, and that problem had a name:

Chorus: Rush Hotfoot.

Narrator One: On his way to work in the morning, Rush Hotfoot was always in a hurry and in a bad mood.

Narrator Two: He would do anything to avoid slowing down for Axle Annie's bus.

Narrator Three: Each morning, the kids would say:

Kids: Watch out for Rush Hotfoot, Annie.

Narrator Three: And each morning Axle Annie's reply was the same:

Axle Annie: I've got two hands on the wheel and nerves of steel. I always watch out for that speed grump!

Narrator One: Annie's kids watched out for him too.

Narrator Two: They watched while Annie drove up, up, up Tiger Hill.

Narrator Three: They watched while they sang their favorite songs.

Kids: *(Sing.)*
The wheels on the bus go round and round,
Round and round,
Round and round.

Narrator One: And they waited for their turn at the Great Gulping Gulch Bridge.

Narrator Two:	The bridge was so narrow that vehicles coming from opposite directions had to take turns driving across.
Narrator Three:	Whenever the kids saw Rush's car in the distance, they'd yell.
Kids:	Here comes Rush! He's bearing down fast! He's driving full blast!
Narrator One:	Then …
Chorus:	BLAAAAAAAAAT!
Narrator One:	Rush's horn would blare as he sped past, while the kids shouted reports on the ridiculous things he was doing while he was driving.
Kids:	Rush Hotfoot is brushing his teeth! Rush Hotfoot is shaving! Rush Hotfoot is plucking his nose hairs!
Narrator Two:	Axle Annie would shake her head.
Axle Annie:	You kids be extra careful getting on and off this bus.
Narrator Three:	One day as Annie approached a railroad crossing, the kids called out their usual warning.
Kids:	Here comes Rush! Bearing down fast! Driving full blast!
Chorus:	BLAAAAAAAAAT!
Narrator One:	went Rush's horn when he saw Annie's flashing lights.
Chorus:	SCREEEEEEEECH!
Narrator Two:	went his brakes when her stop-sign arm swung out.
Rush Hotfoot:	*(Bellow.)* Move that bus, or I'll move it for you!
Narrator Three:	Then, just before Tiger Hill, Rush zoomed past. The kids saw him changing out of his pajamas into his work clothes.
Kids:	*(Chant.)* We see London, we see France!
Axle Annie:	*(Groan.)* Don't tell me.
Kids:	Purple underpants!
Narrator One:	That speed grump made Annie grumpy too! So grumpy that she did something she thought she never would.
Narrator Two:	She attended a meeting of the Burskyville Grouch and Grump Club.

Narrator Three:	And whom should she meet there but Rush Hotfoot himself.
Narrator One:	Rush Hotfoot scowled at Annie.
Rush Hotfoot:	What do YOU have to be grumpy about?
Axle Annie:	I'm grumpy about you, Rush Hotfoot. You ruin my mornings.
Rush Hotfoot:	Oh no. Your BUS ruins MY mornings with its flashing lights and stupid stop-sign arm. Your KIDS ruin MY mornings with their sappy singing!
Kids:	*(Sing.)* The wheels on the bus go round and round, Round and round, Round and round.
Narrator Two:	The other grouches told Axle Annie that she wasn't grumpy enough for them.
Narrator Three:	Being grumpy about Rush Hotfoot didn't count, because Rush Hotfoot would make ANYBODY grumpy! They all drank a gripe-juice toast to him.
Chorus:	Three cheers for Rush! Hiss-Hiss-Boo! Hiss-Hiss-Boo! Hiss-Hiss-Boo! The best bus driver in Burskyville got grumpy because of you!
Narrator One:	The next day a kid with a sprained ankle was struggling onto Annie's bus when he heard a familiar rumble.
Kids:	Watch out for Rush, Annie. He's bearing down fast. Driving full blast!
Axle Annie:	I've got two hands on the wheel and nerves of steel. I always watch out for that speed grump!
Narrator Two:	But while Annie's lights were still flashing and her stop-sign arm was still out, Rush Hotfoot roared past the bus.
Narrator Three:	His wheels spat gravel. Axle Annie was outraged.
Axle Annie:	Rush Hotfoot is worse than a speed grump. He is a major danger! This time he broke the law.
Narrator One:	She radioed her supervisor, who called the police, and soon Rush was pulled over by an officer.

Narrator Two:	Just as the police officer wrote up a ticket for Rush, Axle Annie drove by, her kids singing merrily.
Kids:	*(Sing.)* The wheels on the bus go round and round, Round and round, Round and round.
Narrator Three:	Now Rush Hotfoot was grumpier than ever.
Narrator One:	He caught up with Annie's bus again halfway up Tiger Hill.
Kids:	Watch out, Annie. Here comes Rush!
Axle Annie:	He can't pass on a hill.
Narrator Two:	But Rush blasted past Annie's bus, up and over Tiger Hill, and on toward the Great Gulping Gulch Bridge.
Kids:	*(Yell.)* He was drinking coffee!
Narrator Three:	Rush saw a truck approaching the bridge from the opposite direction.
Narrator One:	He was in too big a hurry to wait for his turn to cross, so he sped up to beat the truck.
Narrator Two:	Just then his cell phone rang.
Chorus:	Brrrrrrrrrrring!
Narrator Three:	He reached for it and knocked hot coffee into his lap.
Rush Hotfoot:	*(Shriek.)* Yeeeeeeeowwwwww!
Narrator One:	Rush's car spun out of control.
Chorus:	SCREEEEEEEEEEECH! BONKETY-BONK-BONK!
Narrator Two:	Rush's car bounced off a guardrail on one side of the bridge, then …
Chorus:	CR-R-R-ASH!
Narrator Three:	It smashed into the other side.
Narrator One:	When Axle Annie arrived at the bridge, she saw Rush's car, tangled in the railing, dangling over Great Gulping Gulch.
Narrator Two:	Rush was holding on for dear life.
Narrator Three:	Annie saw the truck approaching from the other direction.

Axle Annie:	What if the truck driver doesn't notice Rush's car? What if he smashes into the car and sends it hurtling down into Great Gulping Gulch? I have to figure out a way to save Rush!
Narrator One:	Annie maneuvered her bus as close to Rush's car as she could without endangering her kids.
Narrator Two:	She turned on her hazard lights and her white strobe light and her red emergency lights.
Narrator Three:	Her stop-sign arm swung out automatically, and Annie blared her horn while the kids yelled out their windows to the truck driver.
Kids:	*(Yell.)* Watch out for Rush!
Narrator One:	The truck stopped just in time!
Narrator Two:	It took two tow trucks and an emergency helicopter to rescue Rush Hotfoot.
Narrator Three:	Annie's kids sang their favorite songs to him while he waited, to take his mind off being scared.
Kids:	*(Sing.)* The wheels on the bus go round and round, Round and round, Round and round.
Narrator One:	Rush's car was a wreck, and he lost his driver's license.
Narrator Two:	From then on, he rode a tricycle to work.
Narrator Three:	He wore a safety helmet with flashing lights and a special swing-out stop-sign arm.
Narrator One:	Everybody had to slow down for Rush Hotfoot.
Narrator Two:	Rush thought the safest place to be was behind Axle Annie's big yellow bus.
Narrator Three:	After all, Axle Annie had both hands on the wheel and nerves of steel …
Kids and Chorus:	and she always watched out for speed grumps.

The End

Axle Annie and the Speed Grump Activities

Social Studies Connections

Interview a School Bus Driver

Axle Annie is the beloved school bus driver of Burskyville. Learn more about her by reading *Axle Annie* by Robin Pulver (Dial, 1999).

Now, if you have bus drivers for your school, invite one or more of them to come visit your classroom, read *Axle Annie and the Speed Grump* to your students, and share their personal bus-driving experiences.

Introduce students to interviewing. Explain that an interview is a special, formal way of having a conversation in which one or more people ask questions and one person, the interviewee, answers them. Refer students to the Rules for Interviewing on p. 18. Ask them to prepare a set of interview questions for each visitor, which you will forward to him or her in advance of the visit. Be sure to include questions about bus manners and road manners.

If you have city bus drivers in your city, you might consider inviting one of them as well so that students can look for similarities and differences.

> **History Standards**
>
> **Grades K–4 History**
>
> - Understands family life now and in the past, and family life in various places long ago
>
>   – Understands family life in a community of the past and life in a community of the present (e.g., roles, jobs, communication, technology, style of homes, transportation, schools, religious observances, cultural traditions)

> **Life Skills Standards**
>
> **Thinking and Reasoning Standards**
>
> - Effectively uses mental processes that are based on identifying similarities and differences
>
> **Language Arts Standards**
>
> **Listening and Speaking**
>
> - Uses listening and speaking strategies for different purposes

Language Arts Connections

Bad Driver on the Road

Rush Hotfoot is a rude and terrible driver. After reading the story together as a class, ask students to brainstorm the many examples of Rush's bad driving behavior. Using the Bad Driver on the Road graphic organizer on p. 19, suggest one or more alternative behaviors that would be more appropriate for each example of bad behavior.

> **Language Arts Standards**
>
> **Reading Standards**
>
> - Uses reading skills and strategies to understand and interpret a variety of literary texts
>
> **Behavioral Studies Standards**
>
> - Understands conflict, cooperation, and interdependence among individuals, groups, and institutions

Good Driving

After you and your students have discussed Rush Hotfoot's poor driving practices, ask them to brainstorm a list of reasons to be careful drivers. Then, instruct students to choose three supporting arguments for safe driving. Using the Good Driving graphic organizer on p. 20, ask students to write their topic sentence on the seat of the stool, then list one argument/support for their topic sentence on each leg of the stool. Their concluding sentence should be recorded on the rug beneath the stool. Invite students to construct a persuasive paragraph about being a good driver from their graphic organizer.

Language Arts Standards

Writing Standards

- Uses the general skills and strategies of the writing process

- Uses the stylistic and rhetorical aspects of writing

Life Skills Standards

Thinking and Reasoning Standards

- Understands and applies the basic principles of presenting an argument

---

Be a Star Bus Passenger

The students on Axle Annie's school bus are excellent bus riders. After your class has had a chance to interview one of your district's bus drivers and after discussing proper bus behavior, ask students to design a series of illustrated Be a Star Bus Passenger posters which can be laminated and posted on school buses as well as in the halls of the school.

If you'd like to emphasize public speaking skills, invite students to visit other classrooms and present the contents of their posters (and perhaps share the story of *Axle Annie and the Speed Grump* to classes of younger children).

Language Arts Standards

Listening and Speaking

- Uses listening and speaking strategies for different purposes

Writing Standards

- Uses the general skills and strategies of the writing process

- Uses the stylistic and rhetorical aspects of writing

Behavioral Studies Standards

- Understands conflict, cooperation, and interdependence among individuals, groups, and institutions

Life Skills Standards

Self-Regulation

- Considers risks

Music Connections

"The Wheels on the Bus"

Begin by sharing one or more picture book versions of "The Wheels on the Bus" song:

- *The Seals on the Bus* by Lenny Hort, illustrated by G. Brian Karas. Henry Holt & Company, 2000.

- *The Wheels on the Bus* by Nadine Bernard Westcott. Little, Brown, and Company, 2004.

- *The Wheels on the Bus* by Paul O. Zelinsky. Dutton Children's Books, 1990.

Engage students in learning and singing "The Wheels on the Bus" as Axle Annie's students do in the Reader's Theater version of *Axle Annie and the Speed Grump*. The words and a .midi file of the music can be found at www.niehs.nih.gov/kids/lyrics/wheels.htm.

Now, invite students to get creative with the words as a class. Keeping in mind the details of the story, ask them to create additional lyrics for the song to reflect the events of *Axle Annie and the Speed Grump*.

<u>Arts Standards</u>

Music Standards

- Understands the relationship between music and history and culture

<u>Writing Standards</u>

- Uses the stylistic and rhetorical aspects of writing

<u>Life Skills Standards</u>

Working with Others Standards

- Contributes to the overall effort of a group

Rules for Interviewing

1 Set up a time for the interview in advance.

2 Be respectful of the person you are interviewing at all times.

3 Explain the reason for the interview.

4 Ask one question at a time and listen thoughtfully to the answer.

5 Ask for clarification if you don't understand a response.

6 Take your time to record each answer on the interview sheet before asking the next question.

7 Thank the person you have interviewed for spending time answering your questions.

Read! Perform! Learn! 2 Axle Annie and the Speed Grump

Bad Driver on the Road

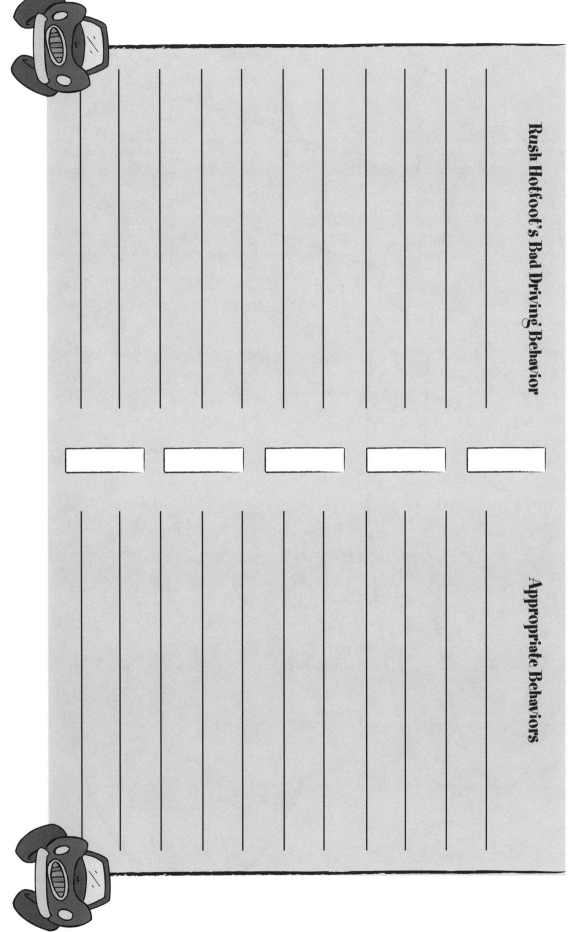

Rush Hotfoot's Bad Driving Behavior

Appropriate Behaviors

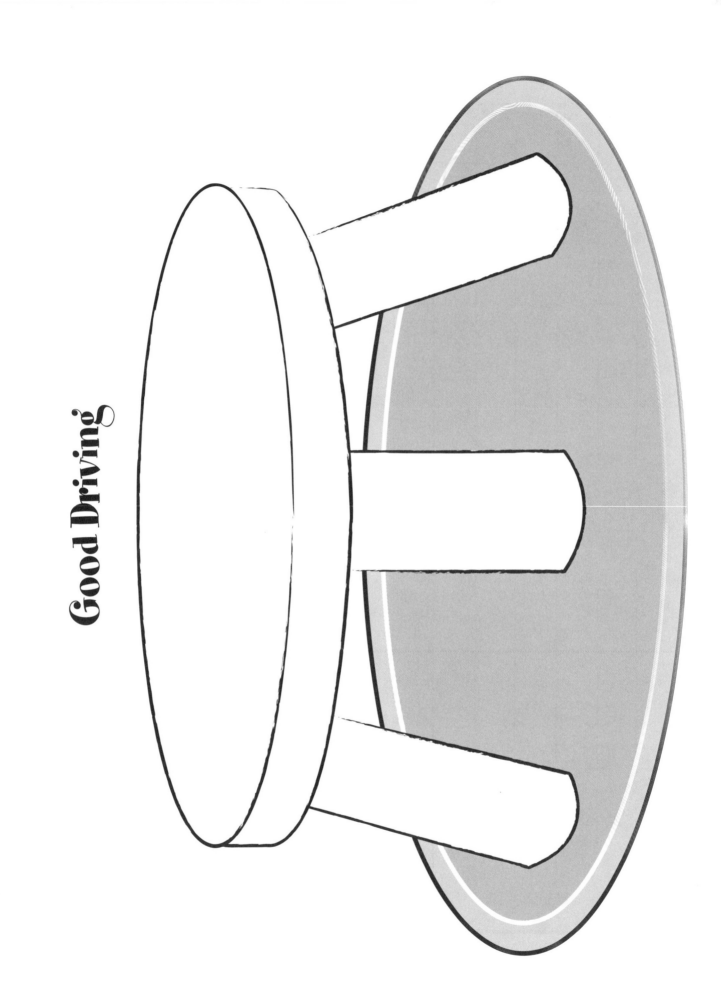

Good Driving

Read! Perform! Learn! 2 Axle Annie and the Speed Grump

Bee-bim Bop!

Read *Bee-bim Bop!* and the interview with Linda Sue Park below to familiarize yourself with the book and the author. Then, hand out a set of photocopied scripts to eight children. (**Note:** Although the main character in the illustrations is a girl, feel free to assign the part to a child of either gender.) Ask the remaining children to be the audience. Have performers face the audience and simply read their parts on the first run-through. Once all readers are comfortable with their parts, have a second reading with the opportunity to use props if desired, and to act out the story while reading. You may want to enhance the performance by staging it in a cooking space with someone preparing bee-bim bop as the reader's theater is read.

Meet Linda Sue Park

Linda Sue Park is the Newbery Medal-winning author of *A Single Shard* and several other middle grade novels, the most recent of which is *Archer's Quest*. She has also written several picture books. Awards for her work include the Jane Addams Honor citation for *When My Name Was Keoko;* the Chicago Tribune Young Adult Fiction Award for *Project Mulberry;* and the James and Irma Black Honor (Bank Street book award) for *The Firekeeper's Son*. Ms. Park lives with her family in Rochester, New York.

Your story makes me hungry! I can just smell the steamy rice, the frying eggs, onions, and meat as I read. What is your personal connection to bee-bim bop? Any stories to tell?

LSP: I don't know any Koreans or Korean-Americans who don't love *bee-bim bop!* My mom made it often when I was growing up; it was on the menu at every Korean celebration or gathering my family ever went to; and I make it for my own family now.

As we read *Bee-Bim Bop!* it's easy (and entirely incorrect, I'm sure) to imagine that this lively verse hopped right off of your pen in its free and easy form. Will you

please talk about the writing of this rhymed verse and any struggles you may have had with form or language?

LSP: It started with the sound of the word itself—it's always seemed to me like such a fun word to say. The first verse did come to me pretty easily ... and when I went on to the second, I realized right away that I was going to have a problem: I'd have to find a whole bunch of words to rhyme with 'bop'! But I found it a fun and interesting challenge. I wrote and discarded many verses before I settled on those that made the final cut.

In terms of language: Just a few years ago, the Korean government officially standardized the romanization of the Korean alphabet; up until then, there was a difficult academic system (McCune-Reischauer), or else people just sort of 'winged it.' Now the approved spelling in English is 'bibim bap.' But when I 'test drove' that spelling on dozens of native English speakers, their pronunciation was invariably incorrect. I opted for a more phonetic spelling, which gets readers closer to the Korean pronunciation. It was not an easy decision to make—because it looks "wrong" if you know the new official spelling—but those are the kinds of choices you sometimes have to make when you're writing multiculturally.

Having won the Newbery Award for *A Single Shard* and having published a strong collection of other novels as well, you are best known for your longer works of fiction. More recently, though, you've stepped into the picture book world as well. What attracts you to the picture book form and what, in particular, do you like about it?

LSP: Two things: I like the change of pace work-wise, and I *love* picture books. I have such admiration for picture books as both an art form and a child's first step into the book world. I consider myself very fortunate to be able to write both novels and picture books.

The main character in your story is such a high-energy child, so eager, so enthusiastic, so HUNGRY! Who was your model for her? Were you a child like her when you were young? If not, what were you like?

LSP: Food is such a huge thing in a young child's life, tangled up with need and pleasure and parents and control and a million other issues. So, on the one hand it's a true universal. On the other hand, in my specific case, my family was and is crazy about food. My mom and dad are both great cooks, and I grew up understanding that good food has the power to bring people together.

It is interesting that your illustrator is Korean. Might you share any information about the selection of an illustrator or the process of working with him and your editor on this book.

LSP: Ho Baek Lee had published one picture book here in the U.S., called *While We Were Out*. It's delightful—about the adventures of a rabbit when his human owners go out for the day. On the strength of that book, Clarion signed him to illustrate the text for *Bee-bim*, and then just a couple weeks later, *While We Were Out* was named a New York Times best illustrated book of the year!

There was one point over which we had some discussion via e-mails through the

editor. He was confused about the egg verse. With most recipes for *bee-bim bop,* you fry one egg per person as a final garnish for the dish, and this is what Mr. Lee is accustomed to. But my mom has always made a flat omelet instead, and cut the omelet into little strips to mix in with everything else. My theory is that the omelet method came into use during hard times, when Korean families might well have found it difficult to obtain one egg per person; the way my mom does it, you can stretch a couple of eggs much further. Once this was explained to Mr. Lee, he understood and drew the omelet instead of fried eggs!

How can readers learn more about you and your books?

LSP: My Web site: www.lindasuepark.com. There's lots of information about me and my books, and about reading and writing, as well as my schedule of appearances. I also keep a blog, mostly about what I've been reading lately: lsparkreader.livejournal.com.

Books by Linda Sue Park

Archer's Quest. Clarion Books, 2006.

Bee-bim Bop! Clarion Books, 2005.

The Firekeeper's Son. Clarion Books, 2004.

The Kite Fighters. Clarion Books, 2000.

Mung-Mung! A Fold-Out Book of Animal Sounds. Charlesbridge, 2004.

Project Mulberry. Clarion Books, 2005.

Seesaw Girl. Clarion Books, 1999.

A Single Shard. Clarion Books, 2001.

What Does Bunny See? A Book of Colors and Flowers. Clarion Books, 2005.

When My Name Was Keoko. Clarion Books, 2002.

Yum! Yuck! A Fold-Out Book of People Sounds. Charlesbridge, 2005.

Bee-bim Bop! Author's Note

Bee-bim bop is a popular Korean dish. Bop is the Korean word for rice, and bee-bim is a nonsense sound meaning "mix-mix." So "bee-bim bop" means "mix-mix rice." It's a favorite meal for many Koreans.

Each diner gets a portion of rice, then tops it with meat, steamed or stir-fried carrots, green vegetables like spinach and mung-bean sprouts, eggs that have been made into flat omelettes and then shredded, and kimchee (pickled cabbage). When all the food is on the plate, you bee-bim—toss and mix everything together like crazy—to make a colorful and delicious meal.

Bee-bim Bop! Script

Roles
Main Character   Mama   Narrator One
Narrator Two   Chorus (four readers)

Narrator One:	Almost time for supper
Mama:	Rushing to the store
Main Character:	Mama buys the groceries— more, Mama, more!
Main Character:	Hurry, Mama, hurry
Mama:	Gotta shop shop shop!
Main Character:	Hungry hungry hungry
Chorus:	for some BEE-BIM BOP!
Narrator Two:	Home and in the kitchen
Mama:	Eggs to stir and fry
Main Character:	Mama, catch the spatula— flip the eggs high!
Main Character:	Hurry, Mama, hurry
Mama:	Gotta flip flip flop!
Main Character:	Hungry hungry hungry
Chorus:	for some BEE-BIM BOP!
Narrator One:	Rice is on the boil
Narrator Two:	Bubbling in the pot
Chorus:	White and sticky-lickety Steaming good and hot!
Main Character:	Hurry, flurry rice

Chorus:	Gotta pop pop pop!
Main Character:	Hungry hungry hungry
Chorus:	for some BEE-BIM BOP!
Narrator One:	Mama's knife is shiny
Narrator Two:	Slicing fast and neat
Mama:	Garlic and green onions Skinny strips of meat.
Main Character:	Hurry, Mama, hurry
Mama:	Gotta chop chop chop!
Main Character:	Hungry—very hungry
Chorus:	for some BEE-BIM BOP!
Narrator One:	Spinach, sprouts, and carrots
Mama:	Each goes in a pan
Main Character:	Let *me* pour the water in— yes, I know I can!
Main Character:	Sorry, Mama, sorry
Mama:	Gotta mop mop mop
Main Character:	Hungry—in a hurry
Chorus:	for some BEE-BIM BOP!
Mama:	Bowls go on the table
Narrator Two:	Big ones striped in blue
Main Character:	I help set the glasses out
Mama:	Spoons and chopsticks too.
Main Character:	Hurry, family, hurry
Narrator One:	Gotta hop hop hop!
Mama:	Dinner's on the table
Chorus:	and it's BEE-BIM BOP!
Narrator Two:	Quiet for a moment
Narrator One:	Papa says the grace
Narrator Two:	Everybody says

All:	"Amen"
Narrator Two:	A smile on every face.
Narrator One:	Rice goes in the middle
Narrator Two:	Egg goes right on top
Chorus:	MIX IT! MIX LIKE CRAZY!
All:	Time for BEE-BIM BOP!

The End

Bee-bim Bop! Activities

Language Arts Connections

Food Rhymes

In her author interview, Linda Sue Park explains that it was an interesting challenge to create rhymes for "bee-bim bop." Every other verse required her to come up with such a rhyme. After reading the story aloud, ask students to create a list of rhyming words that Linda Sue Park used.

Next, ask students in small groups to select one or more of the special family, regional, or cultural foods listed by class members during the Many Cultures, Many Foods activity on p. 28. Challenge them to create a list of rhyming words that would be useful if they were writing a rhyming food poem like the one in *Bee-bim Bop!*

If you have an especially enthusiastic class, you may want to choose the word list from one group and create a group poem modeled on *Bee-bim Bop!*

Language Arts Standards

Writing Standards

- Uses the stylistic and rhetorical aspects of writing

Reading Standards

- Uses reading skills and strategies to understand and interpret a variety of literary texts

Life Skills Standards

Working with Others Standards

- Contributes to the overall effort of a group

Feasting Around the World

Engage students in a small research project to discover the variety of prepared/cooked foods eaten by people around the world. Assess the available print resources in the library and online resources your students might use for this project before you begin, as this will help you refine the list of countries you assign to the groups. Be careful to select countries from several continents.

Some useful print resources include:

- Kids in the Kitchen series by Theresa M. Beatty. PowerKids Press, 1999.

- *The World of Food* by Paula S. Wallace. Gareth Stevens, 2003.

Some helpful online resources include:

- "Focus on Ethnic Cuisine." *Sally's Place.* www.sallys-place.com/food/ethnic_cusine/ethnic_cusine.htm

- "Food." *Cool Planet.* www.oxfam.org.uk/coolplanet/kidsweb/wakeup/food.htm?searchterm=food

- "Food from around the World." *TOPICS An Online Magazine for Learners of English.* www.topics-mag.com/foods/special-foods/global-foods.htm

- "Mrs. Salipante's Foreign Food Recipes." *Lakewood High School.* www.lkwdpl.org/lhs/foreignfoods/

Invite students to locate their country in an atlas and then fill in the Feasting Around the World graphic organizer on p. 30 as they complete their research. If possible,

help students locate a photograph of the prepared food they have identified. As a final step, engage students in sharing information about and photographs of the foods they have found.

Asking Questions, Recording Answers

As *Bee-bim Bop!* reveals, every culture, every region of a country, every family has its own special foods and food traditions. Young children who are quite familiar with their own cultural, regional, and familial foods might not yet have realized that these are unique rather than universal. This activity will give students an opportunity to explore their own food traditions.

Begin by introducing (or reviewing) the skill of interviewing. Explain that an interview is a special, formal way of having a conversation in which one person asks the questions and one person answers them. The person asking the questions usually records the answers, either by writing them down (as your students will do) or by recording them using a taping device. Post a list of the Rules for Interviewing (page 18) in the classroom and/or send it home with students. **Note:** For those students who aren't yet academically or developmentally ready to record interview answers in writing, you may arrange for them to audio-record the interview.

Now, invite students to interview family members about foods that are special to their family using the Many Cultures, Many Foods Interview Sheet on pp. 31–32.

Social Studies Connections

Many Cultures, Many Foods

Once you have completed the Asking Questions, Recording Answers activity, at left, with your students, you are ready to introduce Many Cultures, Many Foods, which will give students an opportunity to explore the food traditions of others.

As a class, use the Many Cultures, Many Foods graphic organizer on p. 33 to create a list of the many foods represented

on students' Many Cultures, Many Foods Interview Sheet on pp. 31–32. Record whether each comes from a family tradition, a regional tradition, or a cultural tradition. As you complete the graphic organizer, it is important to be sensitive to cultural differences and to the fact that some students may be living in dual cultures or outside their biologically hereditary culture as a result of adoption, intermarriage, or complex family patterns. The goal of this activity, however, is to celebrate a diversity of cultures in any community.

Behavior Studies Standards

- Understands that group and cultural influences contribute to human development, identity, and behavior

Life Skills Standards

Thinking and Reasoning Standards

- Effectively uses mental processes that are based on identifying similarities and differences

Bee-bim Bop

In addition to studying the illustrations in *Bee-bim Bop!*, Linda Sue Park's Author's Note on p. 23 explains how bee-bim bop is prepared. After sharing the book with your students, discuss the nutritional elements (protein, grain, vegetables) of this Korean dish and how it contributes to health. Then select a day to enjoy this Korean dish by preparing and eating bee-bim bop together.

Health Standards

- Understands essential concepts about nutrition and diet

Feasting Around the World
Graphic Organizer

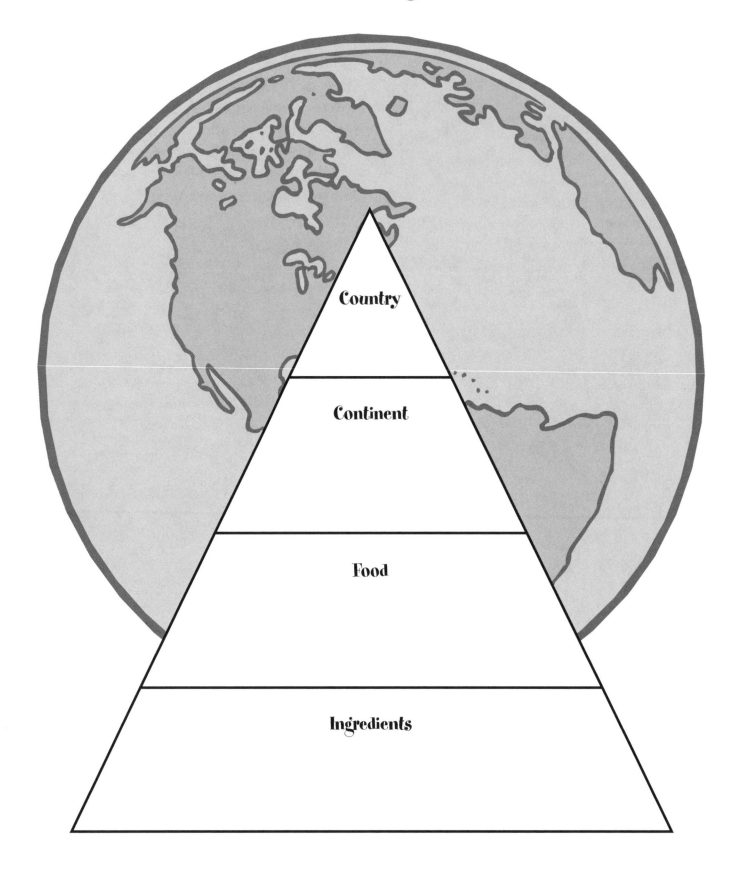

Many Cultures, Many Foods Interview Sheet

Dear Student,

Choose one or more adult members of your family to interview about your family's favorite foods.

1. What foods are special to our family?

_____

- -

_____

_____

- -

_____

2. Did you eat any of these foods as a child?

_____

- -

_____

_____

- -

_____

3. If you ate them when you were a child, were there special times or days to eat them?

_____

- -

_____

_____

- -

_____

4. What are the special foods our family eats at holiday time?

_____

- -

_____

- -

5. Are these foods special to the part of the country we
   live in?

_____

- -

_____

- -

6. Were these foods special to our ancestors?

_____

- -

_____

- -

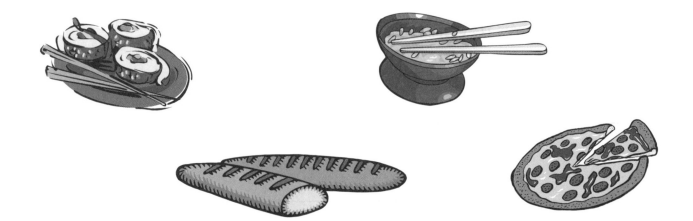

Many Cultures, Many Foods Graphic Organizer

Student Name	Food	Family Tradition	Regional Tradition	Region of the Country	Cultural Tradition	Culture

The Boy Who Drew Birds

Read *The Boy Who Drew Birds* and the interview with Jacqueline Davies below to familiarize yourself with the book and the author. Read the book aloud to children first, so that they can enjoy the illustrations and become familiar with the story. Then, hand out a set of photocopied scripts to nine children. (Note: The parts of the Female and Male Pewee Birds are perfect for challenged readers who need to gain confidence with oral reading.) Ask the remaining children to be the audience. Give readers time to practice their reading until they are fluent. Have performers face the audience and simply read their parts on the first run-through. Once all readers are comfortable with their parts, have a second reading with the opportunity to use costumes or props if desired, and to act out the story while reading.

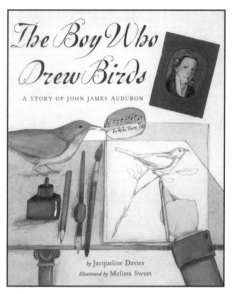

Meet Jacqueline Davies

Jacqueline Davies is the author of six books for children, including *Where the Ground Meets the Sky, The Boy Who Drew Birds, The Night Is Singing, The House Takes a Vacation, The Lemonade War,* and *Tricking the Tallyman.* Her books have won numerous awards and distinctions including the John Burroughs Nature Award, the Sigurd Olson Award for Nature Writing, the NSTA Outstanding Science Trade Book for K–12, the NCSS Notable Social Studies Trade Book for Young People, and the New York Public Library's Books for the Teen Age. Ms. Davies lives in Needham, Massachusetts, with her husband, their three children, and a rambunctious yellow lab named Harley.

Beyond his beautiful and well-known bird paintings and the birding society that bears his name, many of us don't know much about John James Audubon. **What sparked your interest in him initially?**

JD: I came to write about Audubon in a circuitous way. It was actually the birds in the story that interested me at first. I had met a pair of phoebes newly returned to their nest in the spring of 2001, and was fascinated when I learned that the same two birds return to the same nest every year. I wanted to write a picture book about these

birds, but couldn't find a way "in" to the story. Who would be my main character? What would be the main character's motivation? And what would be the problem of the story? While doing research on the birds, I discovered a small footnote related to phoebes: They were the first birds banded in North America, and the banding was done by none other than John James Audubon. From that point on, the story of *The Boy Who Drew Birds* fell into place.

In what ways was John James Audubon like you as a child? Or is he more like you as an adult?

JD: I think it's the rare child who isn't fascinated by the natural world, and like most children I enjoyed poking around in my backyard, collecting rocks and feathers, caterpillars and lightning bugs. I think, however, my strongest connection to Audubon is in our shared dislocation. As a child, I moved five times before the age of ten. Audubon, too, knew what it was like to be the "new kid on the block." When I wrote about him traveling from France to Pennsylvania, not knowing a soul in his new home, I certainly felt a connection to him.

Why did you decide to narrow the scope of your biography of John James Audubon to one year in his life as an adolescent?

JD: Remember, I was interested in the birds before I was interested in Audubon. So it seemed natural to center the story around this single, important experiment that he performed. In writing the book, however, I found that this one year in his life revealed so much about who Audubon was and who he would become. In many ways, I feel that this one episode does indeed tell the larger

story of his life.

Please share some of the fascinating things about John James Audubon that you had to forego including in your story.

JD: Where to begin! He was born in Saint-Domingue and spent the first years of his life in the French Caribbean. The mother who raised him in France was actually a stepmother, and she loved Audubon dearly. For most of his early childhood, Audubon was called Fougère, which is the French word for *fern*. Audubon was a prolific writer who kept journals and wrote letters every day of his life. His writing style was bubbly and overflowing, sometimes melodramatic, always entertaining. When he first began to write in English, his letters were filled with confusing, but charming, malapropisms. I wish there had been room in the book to include some of his effusive lines, such as "I am here in the snairs of the eagle, he will pluck Me a little and then I Shall [sail] on a sheep."

John James Audubon was not only a naturalist and ornithologist, he was an artist of great talent. That makes the art in this illustrated biography particularly important. How do you feel that Melissa Sweet's work enhances your telling of the Audubon story?

JD: Audubon spent his life trying to capture nature, as it existed in the real world, within the pages of his portfolio. Melissa's art is a wonderful salute to this goal of Audubon's. Her paintings—watercolor and collage— are filled with three-dimensional objects found in nature: a pinecone, a porcupine quill, a piece of bark, a nest. These found objects make the paintings themselves

come alive. It is as if the paintings are *breathing*. Nothing would have pleased Audubon more.

How can readers learn more about you and your books?

JD: The best way to learn more about me and my books is to visit my Web site at www.jacquelinedavies.net. I also enjoy visiting schools to talk about my books and the writing life.

Books by Jacqueline Davies

The Boy Who Drew Birds. Houghton Mifflin, 2004.

House Takes a Vacation. Marshall Cavendish, 2007.

Lemonade War. Houghton Mifflin, 2007.

The Night Is Singing. Dial, 2006.

Where the Ground Meets the Sky. Marshall Cavendish, 2004.

About John James Audubon from The Boy Who Drew Birds

Banding a bird—that is, tying a marker around a bird's leg to track its movement—was an innovative idea in Audubon's time. In fact, in 1804, John James became the first person in North America to band a bird. The simple experiment helped prove a complex theory: Many birds return to the same nest each year, and their offspring nest nearby. This behavior is called *homing*. The rest of the world learned of Audubon's experiment when he wrote about it in his book *Ornithological Biography.* Later, in the twentieth century, scientists used bird banding to prove that small birds migrate.

Not long after the story in this book ends, John James returned to France and his father's house. Perhaps he, like the birds, felt a pull toward home. But a year later, he sailed back to America, saying goodbye to Papa Audubon, his "friend through life." It was the last time he saw his father.

The young John James grew to be the greatest painter of birds of all time. He was the first to paint life-size images of birds and the first to show birds hunting, preening, fighting, and flying. His revolutionary paintings pleased two audiences: scientists, who were drawn to their accuracy, and ordinary people who simply enjoyed the beauty of his birds.

Author's Source Note from The Boy Who Drew Birds

In writing this story, I relied primarily on John James Audubon's own account in *Ornithological Biographies* and Shirley Streshinsky's *Audubon: Life and Art in the American Wilderness.* Nearly every detail included in this story is documented in these two books. Audubon did burn many of his early drawings on his birthday. Where he purchased the silver thread is a matter of speculation, but Audubon regularly walked five miles to the nearest village, Norristown, and it is almost certain that Mrs. Thomas, a sober Quaker, would not have any silver thread in her sewing basket. Whether or not Audubon read the works of Aristotle is open to question. Papa Audubon loved to give books as gifts, and it is likely that one of the natural history books he gave to his son included the ancient Greeks' theories on bird migration and hibernation.

Bibliography from The Boy Who Drew Birds

- Audubon, John James. *Writings and Drawings*. Edited by Christoph Irmscher. New York: Library of America, 1999. Includes *Ornithological Biography*; *Myself*; *My Style of Drawing Birds*; and *Mississippi River Journal*.

- Ford, Alice. *John James Audubon*. Norman: University of Oklahoma Press, 1964.

- —, ed. *Audubon, By Himself*. Garden City, N.Y.: Natural History Press, 1969.

- Foshay, Ella M. *John James Audubon*. New York: Henry N. Abrams, 1997.

- Streshinsky, Shirley. *Audubon: Life and Art in the American Wilderness*. New York: Villard Books, 1993.

- Welty, Susan F. *Birds with Bracelets*. Englewood Cliffs, N.J.: Prentice-Hall, 1965.

The Boy Who Drew Birds Script

Roles

John James Audubon	Madame Thomas	Papa Audubon
Aristotle	Narrator One	Narrator Two
Narrator Three	Female Pewee Bird	Male Pewee Bird

Pronunciation

minuet min yoo et´
gavotte gə vot´
Adieu ə doo´
Madame Thomas mə dam´ tō mas´
Il y a des oiseaux eel ee ă´ day wa zō´
musée myoo zā´

Narrator One: It was true that John James could skate, hunt, and ride better than most boys.

Narrator Two: True also that he could dance the *minuet* and *gavotte* as if he had been born a king.

John James: I can fiddle, I can flirt, I can fence.

Narrator Three: But what he liked to do best, from sunup to sundown, was watch birds.

John James: My happiest memories are of woodland walks with my father near our home in France.

Narrator One: On these walks, Papa Audubon would talk of birds.

Papa Audubon: Their colors are so beautiful, their flight so graceful, and—most wonderful of all—their disappearance each fall is so mysterious and their return in the spring so faithful!

Narrator Two: But now John James was eighteen years old and he walked through the Pennsylvania woods alone, his father four thousand miles away.

Narrator Three: Only six months before, his father had put him on a ship.

Papa Audubon: *Adieu!*

Narrator One:	The ship carried John James to America, where he was to live in a farmhouse on the banks of a creek.
Papa Audubon:	I sent my only son there to learn English, to learn commerce, to learn how to make money in America. But mostly I sent him away so that he would not have to fight in Napoleon's war.
John James:	I wonder if I will ever see my Papa again?
Narrator Two:	It was April in Pennsylvania, and slashes of snow still lay in deep hollows. John James splashed across the icy creek.
Narrator Three:	He scrambled up the bank and approached the limestone cave, wondering what he would find today.
John James:	Will it be just the empty nest of a pewee bird, as I have found the last five days? Or will there be—
Female and Male Pewees:	
	Ffh, ffh, ffh!
Narrator One:	A flurry of wings greeted John James.
John James:	The pewee fly-catchers have returned!
Narrator Two:	The female bird flew out of the cave like an arrow shot from a bow.
Female Pewee:	*Ffh, ffh, ffh!*
Narrator Three:	The male bird, larger and darker, beat his wings above John James's head and snapped his beak.
Male Pewee:	*Clack, clack, clack!*
Narrator One:	John James ran out of the cave and crouched next to the creek.
Narrator Two:	He watched as the birds dipped and soared, snapping up mayflies in flight.
John James:	Are these the same pewees who built the nest last year? Where did they spend the winter? Will they return next spring?
Narrator Three:	John James ran home through the woods.
Narrator One:	He burst into the farmhouse kitchen, his words tumbling out in French.

John James:	*(Shout.) Madame Thomas! Madame Thomas! Il y a des oiseaux!*
Narrator Two:	Mrs. Thomas was the housekeeper Papa Audubon had hired to take care of Mill Grove, his American farmhouse.
Narrator Three:	She pointed her long wooden spoon.
Mrs. Thomas:	Off with those muddy shoes!
Narrator Three:	John James quickly took them off and placed them by the fire to dry.
John James:	Birds! I see birds. Two. In cave. Beautiful!
Mrs. Thomas:	*(Frown.)* Birds! Always birds! From the moment you wake up in the morning to the moment you close your eyes at night. You only think about birds. So strange for a boy your age.
Narrator One:	Mrs. Thomas was fond of this energetic French boy. And yet she had to admit that he was something of a cracked pot.
Mrs. Thomas:	Master Audubon, thou wouldst do well to do God's work by tending the farm more and chasing after birds less.
Narrator Two:	But John James, halfway up the narrow staircase, pretended not to hear.
Narrator Three:	He climbed straight to his attic room—his *musée.*
Narrator One:	Every shelf, every tabletop, every spare inch of floor, was covered with nests and eggs and tree branches and pebbles and lichen and feathers and stuffed birds: redwings and grackles, kingfishers and woodpeckers.
Narrator Two:	The walls were covered with pencil and crayon drawings of birds, all signed "JJA."
Narrator Three:	Every year on his birthday, John James took down these drawings—a year's worth of work—and burned them in the fireplace.
John James:	I hope someday I will make drawings worth keeping.
Narrator One:	John James went to his bookcase and took down the natural history books, gifts from his father.
John James:	Where do small birds go in the winter? Do the same birds come back to the same nest each spring?

Narrator Two:	The scientists who wrote these books did not agree; each one gave a different answer.
Narrator Three:	Two thousand years before, the Greek philosopher Aristotle had given the answers to these questions.
Aristotle:	Every fall great flocks of cranes fly south and return in the spring. But small birds do not migrate. Small birds hibernate underwater or in hollow logs all winter.
Narrator One:	Many scientists of the day still agreed with Aristotle.
Narrator Two:	Small birds, they said, gathered themselves in a great ball, clinging beak to beak, wing to wing, and foot to foot, and lay underwater all winter, frozen-like.
Narrator Three:	Fishermen even told stories of catching such tangles of birds in their nets.
John James:	I have never, *ever* found a tangled ball of birds under water. I do not believe everything the scientists say. Why, some of them believe that birds transform from one kind into another each winter! And one scientist claims that birds travel to the moon each fall and return in the spring. Can you imagine? He says the trip takes sixty days!
Narrator One:	John James had never spent much time inside a classroom, and he had failed every exam he had taken in school.
Narrator Two:	But he considered himself a naturalist. He studied birds in nature to learn their habits and behaviors.
John James:	I will bring my books to the cave. And my pencils and paper. I will even bring my flute. I will study my cave birds every day. I will draw them just as they are.
Narrator Three:	And because he was a boy who loved the out-of-doors more than the in, that is just what he did.
Narrator One:	In a week, the birds were used to him.
Narrator Two:	They ignored him as if he were an old stump.
Female and Male Pewees:	
	Fee-bee! Fee-bee!
Narrator Three:	They carried bits of moist mud as he drew with his pencils.

Narrator One: They brought in tufts of green moss as he read his French fables.

Narrator Two: They gathered stray goose feathers from the banks of the creek as he played songs on his flute.

Narrator Three: Soon the dried brown nest had become a soft green bed. And John James had learned to imitate the throaty call of the birds.

Female and Male Pewees:

Fee-bee! Fee-bee!

John James: *Fee-bee! Fee-bee!*

Narrator One: Spring slipped into summer. Summer sighed and became fall.

John James: I watched as two broods of nestlings hatched. I watched as the young birds flew for the first time.

Narrator Two: He began to feel a part of this small family.

Narrator Three: When the days grew shorter and the autumn air began to bite, John James knew the birds would leave soon.

John James: Will they come back in the spring? I have to know!

Narrator One: The question was terribly important to the boy so far from his family.

Narrator Two: In bed that night, he formed a plan. The next day, when the mother and father birds were away from the nest, John James picked up one of the baby birds.

Narrator Three: He had read of medieval kings who tied bands on the legs of their prize falcons so that a lost falcon could be returned.

John James: Why not band a wild bird to find out where it goes? It has never been done, but I'll give it a try.

Narrator One: He pulled a string from his pocket and tied it loosely around the baby bird's leg. The bird pecked it off.

Narrator Two: The next day, he tied another string to the bird's leg. Again the bird pecked it off.

Narrator Three: Finally, John James walked five miles to the nearest village and bought some thread woven of fine strands of silver. This thread was soft and strong. He tied a piece of it loosely to one leg of each baby bird.

John James: My birds have gone!

Narrator One: All winter, John James worked in his *musée*, painting the pencil sketches he had made in the cave.

John James: I hope that on my next birthday, I will have one or two pictures worth saving from the fire.

Narrator Two: The creek was frozen now.

Narrator Three: And each time John James skated past the empty cave, he thought of the two-thousand-year-old question.

Narrators One, Two, and Three:
Where do small birds go, and do they return to the same nest in the spring?

Narrator One: The days grew longer.

Narrator Two: The ice on the creek cracked and melted.

Narrator Three: One morning, John James heard a bird call.

Female Pewee: *Fee-bee! Fee-bee!*

Narrator One: He ran to the cave. He ducked his head and stepped inside.

Narrator Two: The female bird did *not* fly out of the cave like an arrow shot from a bow. The male bird did *not* beat his wings above John James's head and snap his beak.

Narrator Three: Instead, they ignored John James as if he were an old stump. Watching the birds fly in and out of the cave, John James knew that his friends had returned.

John James: But where are last year's babies, now grown? Have they returned, too?

Narrator One: He began to search the woods and orchard nearby, listening for their call.

Narrator Two: Out in the meadow, inside a hay shed, he found two birds building a nest. One wore a silver thread around its leg.

Narrator Three:	Up the creek, under a bridge, he found two more nesting birds. And one wore a silver thread around its leg.
John James:	*(Shout.)* Yes! The same birds return to the same nest! And their children nest nearby.
Narrator One:	But there was no one to hear him.
John James:	I will write to my father. I will tell him what I have learned in America. And when I am older, I will find a way to tell the whole world.
Narrator Two:	He ran back to his house to gather his pencils, paper, and flute.
Narrator Three:	As he ran, he called:
All:	*Fee-bee! Fee-bee!*

The End

The Boy Who Drew Birds Activities

Social Studies Connections

The Life of John James Audubon

The Boy Who Drew Birds examines a small slice of the early life of John James Audubon and conveys his driving passion in life—birds. Once their curiosity is piqued, students may want to know more about this fascinating artist's and ornithologist's life.

After reading *The Boy Who Drew Birds* aloud, also read aloud two other biographies of John James Audubon:

- *Audubon: Painter of Birds in the Wild Frontier* by Jennifer Armstrong. H. N. Abrams, 2003.

- *Into the Woods: John James Audubon Lives His Dream* by Robert Burleigh. Atheneum, 2003.

Then, as a class, create a time line of his life either on paper on a library or classroom wall or using the time-lining function of software such as Kidspiration®. To extend student learning and connections, add well-known local, state, or national dates to the time line.

History Standards

Historical Understanding

- Understands and knows how to analyze chronological relationships and patterns

- Understands the historical perspective

People with Passion

While many famous people are remembered for a solitary contribution to humanity, others are people with a focused life passion that they pursued against all odds over and over again, making multiple contributions in a single field as did John James Audubon with his ornithology. With students, brainstorm a list of famous people who accomplished something great in any area of human endeavor. Conduct research in the library media center to read more about these famous people. You may want to consult the *World Book Student Discovery Encyclopedia* as a quick reference source. Invite students to use the People with Passion graphic organizer on p. 49 to identify the passion of each famous figure and the various ways that it revealed itself in their activities and accomplishments.

History Standards

Historical Understanding

- Understands the historical perspective

Language Arts Standards

Writing Standards

- Gathers and uses information for research purposes

Reading Standards

- Uses reading skills and strategies to understand and interpret a variety of informational texts

Science Connections

The Method of Science

Review or introduce students to the five steps of the scientific method:

1. Name the problem/question.

2. Form a hypothesis and make a prediction.

3. Test your hypothesis.

4. Check and interpret your results.

5. Report your results.

Now, re-read *The Boy Who Drew Birds* and ask students to examine John James Audubon's process for proving his theory that Peewee Flycatchers return to the same nest year after year, a behavior called homing. Record each step of the scientific method as Audubon followed it through.

> ### Science Standards
>
> **Life Sciences**
>
> - Understands relationships among organisms and their physical environment
>
> **Nature of Science**
>
> - Understands the nature of scientific inquiry
>
> - Understands the scientific enterprise

From Here to There: Bird Migration

As Jacqueline Davies writes in her Author's Source Note in *The Boy Who Drew Birds*, "In *Ornithological Biography*, Audubon asserts that Pewee Flycatchers are migratory birds" even though most scientists of the time believed that birds hibernated instead of migrating. Now we know that many species of birds do migrate each year.

Begin by reading this book about bird migration with your students:

- *How Do Birds Find Their Way?* by Roma Gans. HarperCollins, 1996.

Then, in the library media center, use field guides from the reference section or online field guides such as eNature at www.enature.com or All About Birds at www.birds.cornell.edu/AllAboutBirds/BirdGuide/ to select a number of birds who, like the Eastern Phoebe (Pewee Flycatcher) migrate seasonally and ask students to fill out a From Here to There: Bird Migration Information Card (on p. 50) for each. Using a large wall map and many colors of yarn, chart the seasonal migration of these different birds. Attach an Information Card to each strand of yarn.

For intermediate grades students, you may wish to add a viewing of the film *Winged Migration* (available on DVD) to this activity.

> ### Science Standards
>
> **Life Sciences**
>
> - Understands relationships among organisms and their physical environment
>
> **Language Arts Standards**
>
> **Writing Standards**
>
> - Gathers and uses information for research purposes
>
> **Reading Standards**
>
> - Uses reading skills and strategies to understand and interpret a variety of informational texts

Home Sweet Nest

In *The Boy Who Drew Birds*, Audubon discovers that the Peewee Flycatcher birds (now called Eastern Phoebes) lined their nests with bits of moist mud, tufts of green moss, and stray goose feathers from the banks of the creek. Discover, with your students, the materials used in the making of nests by various species of birds from different parts of the country or world.

Begin by reading the following books about bird nests aloud:

- *Birds and Their Nests* by Linda Tagliaferro. Capstone, 2004.

- *Housing Our Feathered Friends* by Dean T. Spaulding. Lerner Publications, 1997.

Then, using field guides from the reference section of the library media center and online resources such as eNature at www.enature.com or All About Birds at www.birds.cornell.edu/AllAboutBirds/BirdGuide/, fill in the Home Sweet Nest graphic organizer (on p. 51) as a class. Discuss how habitat influences the materials available for nest building.

Science Standards

Life Sciences

- Understands relationships among organisms and their physical environment

Language Arts Standards

Writing Standards

- Gathers and uses information for research purposes

Reading Standards

- Uses reading skills and strategies to understand and interpret a variety of informational texts

Audubon Society Visit

If you have an Audubon Society location near you, plan a field trip to visit and learn more about the birds who live in your area. Arrange with the naturalist on the education staff to meet with your students. With students, prepare questions in advance to guide their thinking and experience. If you are unable to visit the Audubon Society with your class, request that a naturalist come to visit your classroom. For a list of locations near you, visit the Audubon Society State Offices and Local Chapter listings at www.audubon.org/states/index.php.

Science Standards

Life Sciences

- Understands relationships among organisms and their physical environment

Language Arts Standards

Listening and Speaking

- Uses listening and speaking strategies for different purposes

Art Curriculum Connections

Classroom Musée

In *The Boy Who Drew Birds* Jacqueline Davies writes:

"He climbed straight to his attic room—his *musée*, he called it. Every shelf, every tabletop, every spare inch of floor was covered with nests and eggs and tree branches and pebbles and lichen and feathers and stuffed birds: redwings and grackles, kingfishers

and woodpeckers. The walls were covered with pencil and crayon drawings of birds, all signed 'JJA.'"

Invite your students to create their own classroom *musée*. First, ask them to collect artifacts from nature such as the ones that Audubon collected and displayed in his *musée*. Try to include dropped bird feathers, abandoned eggs, and abandoned nests (discuss the importance of not disturbing eggs or nests that are being actively tended). Sometimes, nature centers have these natural artifacts to lend to classrooms. Then, study Audubon's own beautiful portraits of birds. If possible, display a sampling of large color photocopies or printed scans of Audubon's portraits on the walls of your *musée*.

Next, work with your art teacher to help students learn the best techniques for drawing and painting birds before asking them to create their own bird portraits. If it is possible for them to sketch live birds, perhaps by visiting a local aviary, zoo, or other nature center, do so. Otherwise, ask them to work from photographs found online. ENature at www.enature.com is a good online source of bird photographs.

Display students' final portraits in your *musée*.

Arts Standards

Visual Arts

- Understands and applies media, techniques, and processes related to the visual arts

Create a Scene in Collage

Illustrator Melissa Sweet employs an illustration technique called collage in which she uses a variety of media, some from the natural world, to create her illustrations for *The Boy Who Drew Birds*. Work with your art teacher to study and learn more about the technique of collage. Invite your students to create an illustrated nature scene using this technique and Sweet's illustrations as a guide. Remind them to include "pieces of nature" in the scene.

Arts Standards

Visual Arts

- Understands and applies media, techniques, and processes related to the visual arts

People with Passion Graphic Organizer

Famous Person	Passion	Activities or Accomplishments that Reveal the Passion

From Here to There: Bird Migration Information Card

Bird: _____

Range: _____

Dates of Spring Migration:

from _____

to _____

Dates of Fall Migration:

from _____

to _____

Bird: _____

Range: _____

Dates of Spring Migration:

from _____

to _____

Dates of Fall Migration:

from _____

to _____

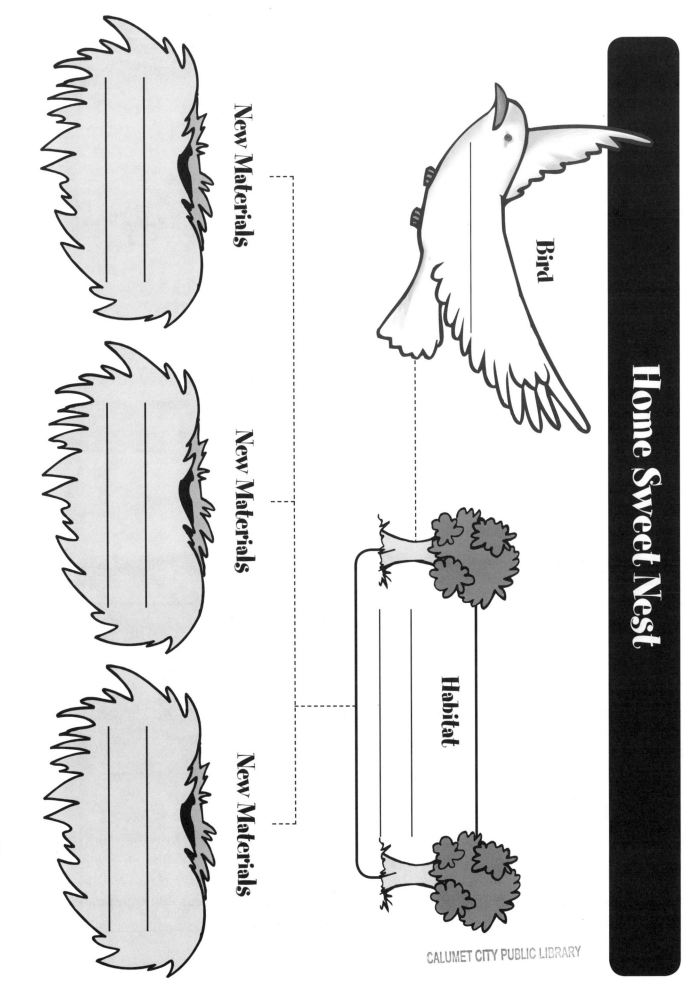

New Materials

New Materials

New Materials

Bird

Habitat

Home Sweet Nest

© 2007 by Toni Buzzeo (UpstartBooks)

The Boy Who Drew Birds **Read! Perform! Learn! 2**   **51**

Button, Bucket, Sky

Read *Button, Bucket, Sky* and the interview with Jacqueline Briggs Martin below to familiarize yourself with the book and the author. Read the book aloud to children first, so that they can enjoy the illustrations and become familiar with the story. Then, hand out a set of photocopied scripts to ten children. (Note that Hector and the Chorus have brief parts that are perfect for challenged readers who need to gain confidence with oral reading.) Ask the remaining children to be the audience. Give readers time to practice their reading until they are fluent. Have performers face the audience and simply read their parts on the first run-through. Once all readers are comfortable with their parts, have a second reading with the opportunity to use costumes or props if desired, and to act out the story while reading.

Meet Jacqueline Briggs Martin

Jacqueline Briggs Martin has always loved the sounds of words. She grew up on a dairy farm in Maine with three brothers and two sisters, received a B.A. from Wellesley College and an M.A. in Child Development from the University of Minnesota. Martin has published 14 books for children, including the ALA Notable book *Grandmother Bryant's Pocket*. Her picture book biography of a self taught scientist—*Snowflake Bentley*, illustrated by Mary Azarian—was awarded the 1999 Caldecott Medal by the American

Library Association. *The Lamp, the Ice, and the Boat Called Fish* was named an ALA Notable Book. Jacqueline Briggs Martin and her husband Richard live in Mount Vernon, Iowa.

Your "Annie Livemore's Oak Tree Notebook," published in *Button, Bucket, Sky*, gives readers very specific directions about growing their own oak trees from acorns. Have you had lots of personal experience in doing it yourself?

JBM: Yes, before the book was published I saved acorns. I picked up hundreds of acorns, did the water test as the books says, and stored the good ones in my refrigerator. During the winter I became busy with other projects and forgot about my acorns.

In the spring I noticed a plastic bag on the back of one of the refrigerator shelves filled with brown. Then I remembered my acorns! Some of them had actually started to sprout. I planted them in buckets and waited for them to grow. Many did. I gave them to friends who wanted oak trees.

Is Annie Livemore modeled on someone from your own life, an older person with a strong reverence for the natural world— and for children?

JBM: Annie Livemore is a person I would like to know, but there is no one person that I thought of as I was writing about her.

Many other of your books include older characters and the children who love them. Please talk about this theme in your books and what has inspired it.

JBM: When I was growing up we lived in the same house as my grandparents. They lived downstairs and we lived upstairs. My grandmother made the best filled cookies I've ever eaten and, though she did not play on the floor with us, was a constant presence in our lives.

A great, great uncle actually lived with us in our apartment. Though his name was Arthur, we all called him "Uncle." I was probably 12 years old before I realized he had another name.

It is so apparent to your readers that you have a deep and abiding love for the natural world, its mystery, and its reliability. In the Caldecott-winning *Snowflake Bentley* you wrote about a real person, Wilson Bentley from Jericho, Vermont. In *Button, Bucket, Sky,* you write about Annie Livemore from Six Penny Road. What do the two have in common with each other—and with you?

JBM: I think Wilson Bentley believed there was something sacred about the beauty of snowflakes. He wanted others to see that beauty and be as awed by it as he was. That does happen when people see his photographs.

Annie Livemore believes in the healing power of trees. Both of these characters, one real, one invented, find inspiration and strength from the beauty and mystery of the natural world. So do I.

When I was young growing up on the farm in Maine I loved to walk down the lane behind the barn, sit in the grove of pine trees at the end of the lane, and listen to the breezes blow through the branches. Now, when I am in a beautiful forest in Maine, a patch of prairie in Iowa, or on the high plains of Tibet, I feel as Wilson Bentley did, that the natural world is a huge temple where we go to be awed by the beauty and remember that we are part of a huge web of life that is more than just people and people's things.

Was Hector a part of the story from the very beginning or did he sneak his way into the story? Why is he there?

JBM: Hector and Annie Livemore were always part of the story. I think in an earlier

version Hector may have actually been a talking cat. I have always loved cats. Our first cat once brought a baby rabbit into the living room in the middle of the night. My husband and I had to get out of bed and rescue that rabbit, which was hiding under the heat registers.

Another cat, which we had when we had small children, loved our children so much that she came down to our living room when she was ready to have her babies and gave birth to five kittens on a bath towel. We were very sad when Whitey was run over by a truck. We no longer have a cat but I still like thinking about them and writing about them.

You are well known for your long, complex, narrative picture books. Yet *Button, Bucket, Sky* is short, simple, and very sweet. What are the rewards or challenges of writing in this shorter format?

JBM: This book took a long time in one sense. I love trees. I grew up in Maine, a state that seems like it's covered in trees except for where people have cut them down. I decided one summer I wanted to write a book about starting trees from seeds. I thought it would be a nonfiction book and include information about oak trees and pine trees. I wrote that book but no publisher wanted to publish it.

So I decided to write a story about starting trees from seeds and focus on oak trees because acorns are so beautiful. (I can never walk past acorns without picking a few up and putting them in my pockets.)

I wrote one version of such a story with Annie Livemore and some greedy cousins. It wasn't very good. I wrote another ver-

sion. Finally I decided I just wanted to write about gathering acorns and planting trees. I knew a boy like Little Sam and I thought the real "Sam" would have liked this tree planting. I wanted him to have a friend so I made up Harriet Grace.

Once I decided on these characters it was a lot of fun to think of the places they might have found the acorns, the containers they might have used, and the places where they might plant the acorns. It was like making a lot of lists. Student writers who don't want to worry about plot could start with this story and add to these lists.

How can readers learn more about you and your books?

JBM: They can visit my Web site at www.jacquelinebriggsmartin.com and they can go to the Web site of the Children's Book Council (www.cbc.org) and look in the archives of About the Author/Illustrator for a column I wrote in 1999 after Mary Azarian won the Caldecott Medal for *Snowflake Bentley.*

Books by Jacqueline Briggs Martin

Banjo Granny with Sarah Martin Busse. Houghton Mifflin, 2006.

Button, Bucket, Sky. Carolrhoda, 1998.

Chicken Joy on Redbean Road. Houghton Mifflin, 2007.

The Finest Horse in Town. Purple House Press, 2003.

Good Times on Grandfather Mountain. Orchard Books, 1992.

Grandmother Bryant's Pocket. Houghton Mifflin, 1996.

Higgins Bend Song and Dance. Houghton Mifflin, 1997.

The Lamp, the Ice, and the Boat Called Fish: Based on a True Story. Houghton Mifflin, 2001.

On Sand Island. Houghton Mifflin, 2003.

Snowflake Bentley. Houghton Mifflin, 1998.

The Water Gift and the Pig of the Pig. Houghton Mifflin, 2003.

Annie Livemore's Oak Tree Notebook from Button, Bucket, Sky

You can grow oak trees too. You will need an adult to help you. First, collect ripe acorns in the fall. They will be brown or purple, not green. Gather more than you think you will need. Pour the acorns into a bucket of water. Throw away the ones that float. Save the ones that sink to the bottom of the bucket. Store your acorns for winter in the refrigerator in plastic bags filled with moist vermiculite or sand.

When spring comes, you can plant your acorns. You will need potting soil, vermiculite, and medium-sized containers (pots, bowls, or buckets) with drainage holes. Fill the containers □ full with potting soil and vermiculite mixed in equal parts. Place several acorns in each pot and cover with ½ to 1 inch of soil. Press the soil gently. Water so the soil is moist but not soggy. Set the pots on a sunny windowsill or porch, or outside in a spot where they will be protected from strong winds and digging animals. Keep the soil moist but not soaked.

The acorns should sprout and begin to grow in a few weeks. (Sometimes they sprout while still in the refrigerator.) Water the seedlings once a week so they do not get too dry. And feed once a month with organic plant food that has been mixed with twice as much water as the label calls for.

When the seedlings are about 6 inches tall, they may need to be moved to larger pots. Gently remove each plant. (If more than one seedling has grown in one pot, carefully separate the plants. Try not to tear the roots.) Plant each seedling in its own pot, using enough soil to fill the pot to the top. Water until the soil is moist, but not muddy. Place in a sunny but protected spot. As the plant grows, water when the soil feels dry, and feed once a month with diluted plant food.

Your oak should be 12 to 14 inches tall to be planted in its permanent home. If your tree is too short when fall comes, set it, in its pot, in the ground. The top of the pot should be level with the surface of the ground. Gently cover the plant with 4 to 6 inches of leaves, grass clippings, or wood chips.

In the spring, when the weather is warm, remove the covering. If your tree is about 12 to 14 inches tall, it can be placed in its permanent home—any spot that has good sun and is not swampy. Remove your tree from its pot and place it in the hole so that the top of the soil around the tree's roots is level with the top of the hole. Fill in the hole with soil. Gently walk on the soil to tamp it down. Water the tree with about one gallon of water.

Place wood chips 4 to 6 inches deep in a circle around your tree trunk. They will help

keep the soil moist and protect your tree. You may want to put a small fence around your tree to protect it from digging by cats and dogs, or other accidents.

Water once a week in dry weather, and feed once a month with an organic fertilizer made with two times as much water as the label calls for.

Enjoy your trees. Perhaps others will see them and decide that they, too, want to hear the music of trees.

Button, Bucket, Sky Script

Chorus:	BUTTON
Narrator One:	Every day was the same in Annie Livemore's small house on Six Penny Road.
Narrator Two:	She ate chicken soup, mended her clothes with thread and buttons, dusted the chairs and the old piano.
Narrator Three:	The best part of each day came when Annie and her cat Hector—
Hector:	Meow!
Narrator Three:	sat outside under their big oak tree.
Annie Livemore:	That tree has its own music.
Narrator One:	Sometimes the two friends napped beneath the rustling leaves.
Narrator Two:	One afternoon Annie Livemore dreamed the oak was sick and she gave it chicken soup, but the soup was no cure.
Narrator Three:	When she woke, she looked up at the tree, the last in the neighborhood, and knew what to do.
Annie Livemore:	Hector, come with me. We're wasting our time with mending and dusting. We are late with our work.
Narrator One:	Hector stretched.
Hector:	Meow!
Narrator One:	He did not love work, but he poked along behind Annie Livemore and watched for a chance to dig holes.
Narrator Two:	They saw Harriet Grace, kicking a stone.

Annie Livemore:	Come with us. We are picking up buttons—shiny brown buttons with oak tree songs inside.
Chorus:	Oak tree songs inside!
Narrator Three:	Harriet Grace was bored with the stone, so she followed along behind Hector.
Hector:	Meow!
Narrator One:	Little Sam was flat on the ground, watching clouds, but he jumped up to join Annie's crew and look for treasures he could hold in his hand.
Narrator Two:	The four walked down Six Penny Road, in and out of town.
Harriet Grace:	I found acorns under a tree where people tacked notes to each other, under a tree where two friends brought milk to a stray kitten. I filled my hat with acorns and didn't want to stop.
Little Sam:	I picked up acorns under a tree where a ladybug walked on my arm, under a tree where clumps of butterflies rested in the fall sun. I filled my pockets with acorns and I thought I would never have enough.
Narrator Three:	Hector dug holes under park benches and picnic tables.
Hector:	Meow!
Annie Livemore:	I picked up acorns under a tree where children ate pickle sandwiches and laughed at riddles, under a tree where a dog ran off with a loaf of bread, under a tree where a man sang a song to a crying baby.
Narrator One:	They brought the acorns to Annie Livemore's porch.
Narrator Two:	Some were long and thin.
Narrator Three:	Others no bigger than a fingernail.
Little Sam:	We are rich with acorns.
Harriet Grace:	They are beautiful as polished pianos.
Narrator One:	Annie got out her big washtub and filled it with water.
Narrator Two:	They poured the acorns into the water and saved the ones that sank to the bottom of the tub.
Narrator Three:	Annie put them in bags of sand and stored them in her cool cellar.

Annie Livemore:	In the spring we'll plant these buttons in buckets and pots.
Chorus:	BUCKET
Narrator One:	When the snow was gone and yards were yellow with dandelions, the children went back to Annie Livemore's.
Little Sam:	All winter, I saved ice cream tubs from the Sweets Shop on Six Penny Road. And I found a teapot with a broken spout.
Harriet Grace:	I brought my father's old workshoe with the scuffed-out toe, my Aunt Lucy's straw hat, and the rusted bucket that had carried toads to school.
Annie Livemore:	I sat on my porch and scrubbed out cracked soup bowls, plant pots, and berry buckets.
Narrator Two:	Hector dug holes in the soft earth under the porch.
Hector:	Meow!
Narrator Three:	The friends put soil into all their tubs, buckets, and bowls—even the shoe.
Narrator One:	They dropped acorns in each and added more soil.
Narrator Two:	After a few weeks the tree seeds sprouted tiny shoots.
Harriet Grace:	The shoots look like toothpicks. I wonder if they'll grow?
Little Sam:	It's a bucket forest for ladybugs and spiders.
Narrator Three:	In the fall they set the buckets, pots, and other planters into the ground and covered them with leaves and grass.
Narrator One:	In the winter, when it snowed, and the air was so cold birds wouldn't fly, Little Sam worried.
Little Sam:	What if the trees freeze?
Harriet Grace:	We could put down blankets.
Annie Livemore:	The leaf cover will be enough.
Narrator Two:	And in the spring, when they raked away the leaves and grass, they found their tiny trees.
Narrator Three:	For another year the trees grew and the children grew. Harriet Grace climbed an apple tree.
Harriet Grace:	Look! I'm a giant.

Narrator One:	She watered the trees and told them stories.
Narrator Two:	Little Sam built bird houses and bird feeders.
Narrator Three:	He gave the trees plant food and sang songs to them.
Chorus:	SKY
Narrator One:	It was the third spring.
Annie Livemore:	It's time to plant our trees.
Narrator Two:	Annie, Harriet Grace, Little Sam, and Hector walked along Six Penny Road looking for places where oak trees could grow.
Narrator Three:	Hector dug all the holes.
Hector:	Meow!
Little Sam:	I planted trees where there were neighbors to carry water in jelly jars, where people would go out in slippers in the early morning to see if a tree had grown.
Harriet Grace:	I planted oaks in lonely places that needed the songs of tree-hopping birds, in noisy places that needed trees to quiet the bustle of cars and trucks.
Annie Livemore:	Hector and I planted trees where children would roll and run and carry acorns home in their pockets, in places where people would come with cousins and picnic baskets.
Chorus:	The years went by.
Narrator One:	Annie Livemore, Hector, and their friends went out many times to gather acorns.
Narrator Two:	Hector dug dozens of holes.
Hector:	Meow!
Narrator Three:	The trees on Six Penny Road, trees in and out of town, grew into the sky.
Narrator One:	Little Sam and Harriet Grace learned to hear the music of nesting birds and rustling leaves.
Chorus:	More seasons passed.
Narrator Two:	Annie Livemore grew very, very old.
Narrator Three:	And Hector was the oldest cat under the sun.

Hector:	Meow!
Narrator One:	One fall day while napping under their favorite tree, they were awakened by Little Sam (no longer little) and Harriet Grace.

Harriet Grace and Little Sam:

Hello! We have brought our families and best friends back to Six Penny Road to walk among the trees and pick up acorns. These are buttons with oak tree songs inside. We will plant them and wait to hear the music of trees.

Narrator Two:	Annie Livemore smiled.
Narrator Three:	And so did the oldest cat under the sun.
Hector:	Meow!

The End

Button, Bucket, Sky Activities

Science Curriculum Activities

Grow Your Own Oak Trees

In *Button, Bucket, Sky,* Jacqueline Briggs Martin includes "Annie Livemore's Oak Tree Notebook" in which she explains how to grow oak trees from acorns. Invite your students to grow oak trees following Annie Livemore's instructions. If you live in a part of the country where oak trees do not grow, replace the acorns with other nuts or seeds from your local trees.

While this is a springtime classroom project, it must begin in the fall, so you may want to read the book and gather the acorns, nuts, or seeds then. Remind students periodically that they are on hand for spring planting!

> **Science Standards**
>
> **Life Science Standards**
>
> - Understands the structure and function of cells and organisms
>
> - Understands relationships among organisms and their physical environment

Arts Curriculum Activities

Grow a Pumpkin from an Oak

Acorns provide other opportunities for fun, beyond the important lesson of growing trees from them. In fact, if you have an abundant source of acorns in your neigh-borhood, challenge your students to gather enough of them for both growing trees and transforming them into pumpkins!

Begin by either freezing or baking in a slow oven the acorns that you will use for this craft (but be sure **not** to bake or freeze the acorns you will use to grow trees). The freezing or baking will kill all weevils who have moved in to the acorn, feasted on the nutmeat, and are just about ready to emerge into the world.

Next, remove the caps and invite students to paint the acorns orange using acrylic paint and either a brush or a dipping method. When the acorns have dried, use a fine brush or fine-tipped permanent marker to add jack-o'-lantern faces.

> **Arts Standards**
>
> **Visual Art Standards**
>
> - Understands and applies media, techniques, and processes related to the visual arts

"The Acorns on the Oak"

Challenge students to rewrite the classic children's song "The Wheels on the Bus" as "The Acorns on the Oak" based on their reading of *Button, Bucket, Sky* as well as their learning about oak tress and acorns.

Begin by reviewing the song "The Wheels on the Bus." The words and a .midi file of the music can be found at www.niehs.nih. gov/kids/lyrics/wheels.htm. Tell students

that as they learn more about oak trees during the class exploration, they should be listening for facts they can embed in a similar song about oak trees.

Next, extend student learning about oak trees. Research the oak tree online at About Oak Trees at www.about-oak-trees.com. You may also want to share other books with your students. For primary grades, consider *From Acorn to Oak Tree* by Jan Kottke (Children's Press, 2000). Slightly older students will enjoy *Oak Tree* by Gordon Morrison (Houghton Mifflin, 2000). Finally, as a group, create the song "The Acorns on the Oak" and sing it together.

Arts Standards

Music Standards

- Understands the relationship between music and history and culture

Language Arts Standards

Reading Standards

- Uses reading skills and strategies to understand and interpret a variety of informational texts

Writing Standards

- Uses the stylistic and rhetorical aspects of writing

- Gathers and uses information for research purposes

Life Skills Standards

Working with Others Standards

- Contributes to the overall effort of a group

Language Arts Curriculum Activities

Nature Has Its Own Music

Annie Livemore uses an abstraction when she says, "The tree has its own music." Begin by asking students what they think Annie means. Once they understand that she is comparing the sound of rustling leaves to music, they are ready to understand what an abstraction is (a comparison between two things that have a major identifying aspect in common). Invite students to think of other nature abstractions. What might each natural thing they select be compared to? Ask students to focus on comparisons that involved the other senses, such as the fields (of fog) that "have their own smoke" and sparkling oceans that "have their own diamonds."

Using the Nature Has Its Own Music abstracting graphic organizer on p. 66, ask students to create a list of original nature abstractions.

Language Arts Standards

Writing Standards

- Uses the general skills and strategies of the writing process

- Uses the stylistic and rhetorical aspects of writing

- Gathers and uses information for research purposes

Life Skills Standards

Thinking and Reasoning Standards

- Effectively uses mental processes that are based on identifying similarities and differences

Nature Music Poems

Begin by creating class poems from the abstractions once students have completed the Nature Has Its Own Music graphic organizer on p. 66. Ask students to cluster their abstractions by classifying the elements of nature they have used. [**Note:** Some classification strategies might be by ecosystem, by size, by living/nonliving, etc.] Use the classifying itself as an opportunity to engage students in complex thinking.

Invite students to create group poems by crafting an introductory and concluding line to surround a list of abstractions classified together. Once students are comfortable with the process, ask them to create individual nature abstraction poems, focusing on a single sense, single ecosystem, or some other organizing principle.

<u>Language Arts Standards</u>

Writing Standards

- Uses the general skills and strategies of the writing process

- Uses the stylistic and rhetorical aspects of writing

<u>Life Skills Standards</u>

Thinking and Reasoning Standards

- Effectively uses mental processes that are based on identifying similarities and differences

<u>Life Skills Standards</u>

Working with Others Standards

- Contributes to the overall effort of a group

Social Studies Curriculum Activities

The Trees in Your Community

As she describes Annie Livemore, Harriet Grace, and Little Sam traveling down Six Penny Road, in and out of town to find their acorns, Jacqueline Briggs Martin creates a sense of the community where they live and what people's lives there are like. As they searched, they found acorns under oak trees that marked special places in their community, places where all sorts of wonderful things had happened. Discuss what sort of community and town Annie Livemore, Harriet Grace, and Little Sam live in by looking at the places they found acorns:

"where people tacked notes to each other" (Harriet Grace)

"under a tree where two friends brought milk to a stray kitten" (Harriet Grace)

"where a ladybug walked on my arm" (Little Sam)

"under a tree where clumps of butterflies rested in the fall sun" (Little Sam)

"where children ate pickle sandwiches and laughed at riddles" (Annie Livemore)

"under a tree where a dog ran off with a loaf of bread" (Annie Livemore)

"under a tree where a man sang a song to a crying baby" (Annie Livemore)

Invite students to think about the small, special things that might have happened under a tree near their house or in their community. Use The Trees in Your Community graphic organizer on p. 67 to

draw the events or write a phrase similar to the ones above. Ask students to share their ideas and lead a discussion about what their ideas say about what is important in their community.

<u>**History Standards**</u>

Grades K–4 History Standards

Topic 1—Living and Working Together in Families and Communities, Now and Long Ago

- Understands the history of a local community and how communities in North America varied long ago

<u>**Behavioral Studies Standards**</u>

- Understands that group and cultural influences contribute to human development, identity, and behavior

<u>**Life Skills Standards**</u>

Working with Others Standards

- Works well with diverse individuals and in diverse situations

Nature Has Its Own Music
Graphic Organizer

Something in Nature	Attribute	Caused By ...
tree	**music**	rustling leaves
fields	**smoke**	fog
ocean	**diamonds**	sparkling waves

The Trees in Your Community
Graphic Organizer

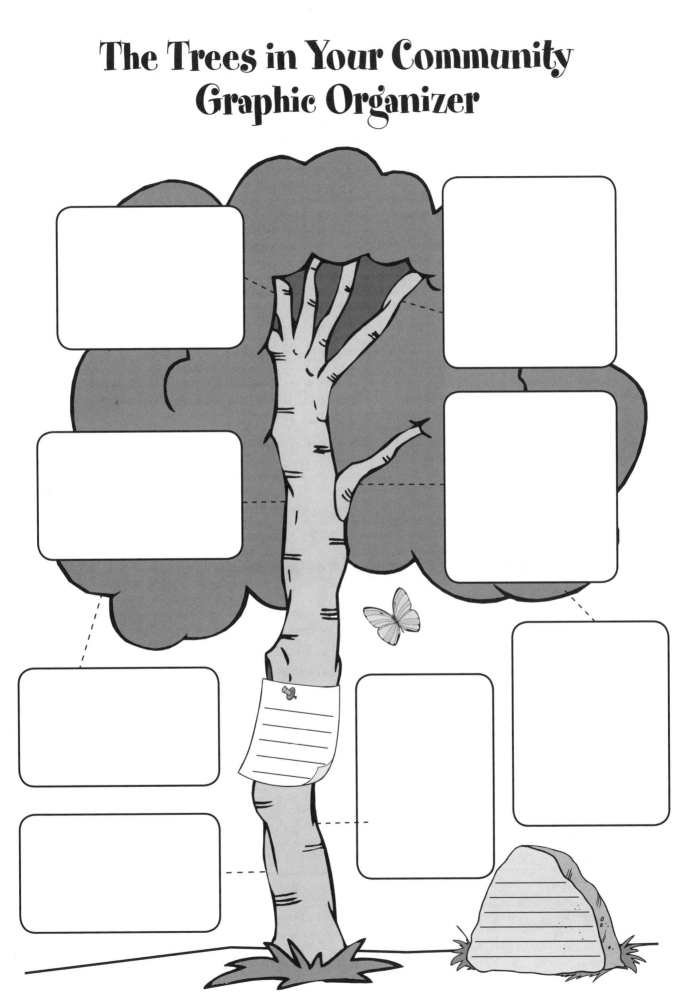

Even Firefighters Hug Their Moms

Read *Even Firefighters Hug Their Moms* and the interview with Christine Kole MacLean below to familiarize yourself with the book and the author. Read the book aloud to children first, so that they can enjoy the illustrations and become familiar with the story. Then, hand out a set of photocopied scripts to fifteen children. Ask the remaining children to be the audience (or if your class is relatively small, make the chorus bigger and involve them all). Have performers face the audience and simply read their parts on the first run-through. Once all readers are comfortable with their parts, have a second reading with the opportunity to use props or costumes—such as hats, if desired—and to act out the story while reading.

Note: Hat patterns are available at www.tonibuzzeo.com/evenfirefightershats.pdf.

Meet Christine Kole MacLean

Christine Kole MacLean has been a professional writer and editor for twenty years. Inspired by her children, she began writing juvenile fiction in 2001. Her first picture book, *Even Firefighters Hug Their Moms,* was highlighted in *Time* magazine and *USA Today.* Scholastic recently selected her first novel for children, *Mary Margaret and the Perfect Pet Plan,* for its book fairs and clubs. Two more novels about Mary Margaret and a young adult novel are forthcoming. Christine lives with her husband and two children in West Michigan. Find out more at www.christinekolemaclean.com.

What was your inspiration for *Even Firefighters Hug Their Moms?* One can't help but wonder if your personal experience is that of the mom!

CKM: It absolutely is. One morning my then four-year-old son raced through the kitchen wearing his fireman's helmet, rain slicker, and a Tigger backpack, to which he had attached the vacuum cleaner hose. I asked him for a hug. "Too busy fighting fires," he said. And I thought, a little wistfully, "Even firefighters hug their moms." I immediately thought

it was a good idea for a picture book and I jotted the phrase down in my journal. That book will always have a special place in my heart because essentially it's a snapshot of the way we spent our days when my children were young.

Part of the work of writing a story like *Even Firefighters Hug Their Moms* is deciding which careers you will include and which you won't. What were some of the careers you considered but didn't include? Please reflect on the things that helped you to make your choices and the role that potential illustration opportunities played.

CKM: To begin with, I simply chose my son's favorites. The firefighter, police officer, and garbage truck driver were his top three. (For about four years, my living room looked like the "garbage truck" scene in the book—and I'm not exaggerating!) After my editor accepted the book, she asked me to add two or three more jobs; she suggested a baseball player and a news reporter, I think. But I thought one of the appealing elements—to boys like mine, at least—was that each job involved big equipment, flashing lights, and loud noises. So I added the train conductor and astronaut scenes.

Were any of Mike Reed's illustrations especially surprising or delightful to you? Did he use household items, furnishings, or architecture in ways you hadn't yet imagined?

CKM: When I was writing the story, I envisioned the boy in the story using common household objects, because that's where kids' imaginations—and all the fun!—come in, and I had shared that with

my editor. Mike added his own ideas, e.g., the wagon as the police car and cardboard box for the rocket. My favorite was his idea to use the ceiling fan for the helicopter blades. It was inspired!

What were you like as a child? Were you highly imaginative like the main character of the story, were you a follow-the-leader younger sibling like the little sister, or were you someone else entirely?

CKM: I'm the youngest of six kids, and I think I followed a lot. It was the only way my brother and sisters would let me play with them. There was a big grove of trees—almost a woods, really—and each of my siblings had built their own "house," which they'd patched together out of leftover lumber. We called the grove "Shanty Town" and we had a general store, a church, and a pet graveyard, in addition to the houses, and we'd play different roles, e.g., store owner or minister.

Usually, I just did what my siblings told me to, a lot like the little girl in the book. Once when I was helping one of my sisters put a roof on her house, she dropped a piece of sheet metal on me, and it cut my head. We had a lot of freedom in Shanty Town, but we also made a lot of trips to the doctor for tetanus shots!

However, I do remember being the star in my own imagination, making up newspaper headlines about myself, such as *Girl Sees Snake, Stifles Scream*. That sort of thing.

If the young Christine were the main character of the story, what are some of the imaginative careers you might have played at?

CKM: I loved horses and had one of my own. Until I was about twelve, when I wasn't riding a horse, I was pretending to be one. Other than that? Horse trainer, jockey, or champion rider. I guess you could say my imagination was narrow and deep rather than broad.

How can readers learn more about you and your books?

CKM: Visit my site—www.christinekolema-clean.com. It has all the usual things, including lesson plans. But the best part of the site is a blog written by one of my main characters, Mary Margaret. She's much funnier than I am. Really. Even my mother says so!

Books by Christine Kole MacLean

Even Firefighters Hug Their Moms. Dutton, 2002.

Everybody Makes Mistakes. Dutton, 2005.

Mary Margaret and the Perfect Pet Plan. Dutton, 2004.

Mary Margaret, Center Stage. Dutton, 2006.

Mary Margaret Meets Her Match. Dutton, 2007.

Even Firefighters Hug Their Moms Script

Big Frank: My name is Big Frank, and I'm a firefighter. Every morning I get up and look at the newspaper to find out where the fires are. Then I get dressed in my protective gear. My air tank and facemask help me breathe even if the smoke is as thick as a milkshake. I climb onto my hook and ladder truck and drive to the fire.

Firefighter Sally: Sometimes I go along with Big Frank.

Big Frank: When we get to the fire, we rush into the burning building, right past Mom.

Mom: How about a hug?

Big Frank: Too busy fighting fires.

Mom: Even firefighters hug their moms.

Officer Dave: My name is Officer Dave, and this is my partner and police dog, Rex.

Rex: Woof!

Officer Dave: We stand guard at the door and when criminals come by I announce it on the loudspeaker and warn everyone.

Officer Dave and Chorus:
Stand back! Criminals coming through.

Officer Dave: Then we lock up all the criminals in jail. My mom walks by. Don't worry about your safety, ma'am. We've got you covered.

Mom: How about covering me with a hug?

Officer Dave:	No time. We've got to serve and protect.
Mom:	Even police officers hug their moms.
Joe:	My name is Joe and I'm an EMT. That's short for "emergency medical technician."
Junior:	I'm Joe's partner. I'm in training.
Joe:	I'm teaching her everything I know. Over the radio we hear about an accident, and we spring into action. We bandage up the man's cuts and scrapes and put him on a stretcher. We give him a bowl of ice cream to make him feel better. Then we race to the hospital. We keep the siren on the whole way.
Chorus:	WEE-oooo, WEE-ooo, WEE-ooo!
Joe:	My mom is waiting in the emergency room when we get to the hospital.
Mom:	Can I have a hug?
Joe:	Trying to save some lives, here.
Mom:	Even ambulance drivers hug their moms.
Joe:	Maybe ambulance drivers do. But I'm an EMT.
Dan:	My name is Dan, and I'm a construction worker. I drive a front loader. I make the yellow light flash.
Chorus:	BEEP! BEEP! BEEP!
Dan:	When I back up, everyone gets out of the way. Sometimes people watch me work.
Chorus:	Can we help?
Dan:	Thanks, but no. Better leave the heavy work to the pros.
Mom:	*(Shout.)* Can you take a coffee break and give me a hug?
Dan:	*(Shout.)* Coffee break's over.
Mom:	Even construction workers hug their moms.
Captain Steve:	I'm Captain Steve, and I'm a helicopter pilot. I work for the Coast Guard. I rescue people off their boats during hurricanes and tornadoes and other gigantic storms. My partner uses a winch to pull them to safety.
Mom:	Can I hug the hero?

Captain Steve:	*(Shakes head no.)* It's just part of the job.
Mom:	Even helicopter pilots hug their moms.
Chorus:	Whop-whop-whop-whop-whop-whop-whop.
Captain Steve:	*(Yell and point up.)* Sorry! I can't hear you!
Dave:	My name is Dave, and I'm the conductor of this train. I call to the people waiting to get on.
Dave and Chorus:	. . . Tickets, please!
Dave:	I take their tickets as they board. One of them tries to sneak a pig onboard. No farm animals! This is a *passenger* train.
Mom:	What do you get when you buy a ticket?
Dave:	You get a train ride to Chicago. Then you get a train ride home.
Mom:	Snacks?
Dave:	No, but you can buy food in the dining car.
Mom:	Hugs?
Dave:	No, no hugs. Only a ride to Chicago.
Mom:	Even conductors hug their moms.
Chorus:	WOO-WOOOOO!
Dave:	All aboard! This train is leaving the station.
Neil:	My name is Neil, and I'm an astronaut. This is my rocket. Yesterday I went to the moon. Don't believe anyone who tries to tell you it's made of cheese. It's made out of rock. Trust me. Today I'm going to Mars. I radio Mission Control.
Neil and Chorus:	Come in, Mission Control. Ready for take off!
Neil:	When they give me the thumbs up, I blast off.
Mom:	What's Mars made of?
Neil:	Legos.
Mom:	I'm surprised you came back.
Neil:	I'm here to get my Lego men, then I'm going back again.

Mom:	Any chance you'll give me a hug first?
Neil:	No.
Mom:	Wait just a minute, Buster. I gave you directions to Mars. A quick hug doesn't seem like too much to ask.
Neil:	*(Shrugs.)* Well, it's a little hard to hug when you're wearing a bulky space suit.
Mom:	Huh. Even astronauts hug their moms.
Rick:	My name is Rick, and I'm a garbage truck driver. I stop at each house and pick up their trash, like worn out toasters, slimy food wrappers, and pacifiers that are bad for the baby's teeth. I turn on the crusher.
Chorus:	Clunk! Whirrrr! Creeeee!
Rick:	It mashes everything down so more trash will fit. Whenever a lady throws something out by mistake, I get it back for her. Sometimes the lady is so happy that she tries to give me a hug. I let her, because …
Chorus:	… even garbage truck drivers hug their moms.
All:	Sometimes.

The End

Even Firefighters Hug Their Moms Activities

Social Studies Curriculum Connections

Community Helpers

Many of the characters in *Even Firefighters Hug Their Moms* are community helpers. Ask students to help you create a list of those who are community helpers with a description of what they do to help the members of the community. Next, add to the list those community helpers who aren't included in the book. What do they do to help members of the community?

Invite a variety of the community helpers on the list to visit your classroom or grade level and talk about their jobs and their contributions to the community.

What Do People Do All Day?

Christine Kole MacLean's book, *Even Firefighters Hug Their Moms* is, in some ways, a career guide because a variety of professions are presented along with the activities that professional engages in that keeps him too busy to hug his mom! After sharing the book, invite groups of students to create a host of additional characters for a companion book. Using a variety of career resources from your library media center, ask students to brainstorm a list of professionals they'd like to feature in a sequel. Instruct them to use the What Do People Do All Day? graphic organizer on p. 79 to identify the job of each character, a likely helper/companion, and the major activities the professional and his or her helper engage in.

History Standards

Grades K–4 History

- Understands family life now and in the past, and family life in various places long ago

  – Understands family life in a community of the past and life in a community of the present (e.g., roles, jobs, communication, technology, style of homes, transportation, schools, religious observances, cultural traditions)

Language Arts Standards

Listening and Speaking

- Uses listening and speaking strategies for different purposes

---

History Standards

Grades K–4 History

- Understands family life now and in the past, and family life in various places long ago

  – Understands family life in a community of the past and life in a community of the present (e.g., roles, jobs, communication, technology, style of homes, transportation, schools, religious observances, cultural traditions)

Language Arts Standards

Writing Standards

- Gathers and uses information for research purposes

Reading Standards

- Uses reading skills and strategies to understand and interpret a variety of informational texts

When I Grow Up

Using the list of careers from *Even Firefighters Hug Their Moms* as well as the additional careers students brainstormed for the What Do People Do All Day? and Community Helpers activities on p. 75, ask students to choose one career they'd like to have when they grow up.

In the library media center, help students research their chosen careers using a variety of books from the nonfiction section, including the Exploring Careers series from KidHaven Press, and online resources (you'll find online links for young students at the Vocational Information Center online at www.khake.com/page64.html). Using a graphic organizer or note cards, ask students to record the primary job responsibilities of the career.

Now, invite each student to create a PowerPoint® slide that explains why he or she wants to pursue the researched career. Establish criteria for the content of the slide including title of the career, primary job responsibilities, and a clear explanation of why he or she thinks it might be a good "fit."

Compile student slides into a single PowerPoint® presentation to share with other grade level classes or parents.

Language Arts Standards

Writing Standards

- Gathers and uses information for research purposes

Reading Standards

- Uses reading skills and strategies to understand and interpret a variety of informational texts

History Standards

Grades K–4 History

- Understands family life now and in the past, and family life in various places long ago

    – Understands family life in a community of the past and life in a community of the present (e.g., roles, jobs, communication, technology, style of homes, transportation, schools, religious observances, cultural traditions)

Life Skills Standards

Thinking and Reasoning Standards

- Understands and applies the basic principles of presenting an argument

Technology Standards

- Knows the characteristics and uses of computer software programs

Where Do People Work?

Review mapping skills including cardinal directions and symbology. Some book resources that might be helpful include:

- *Mapping Penny's World* by Loreen Leedy. Henry Holt & Company, 2000.

- *Me on the Map* by Joan Sweeney. Crown Publishers, 1996.

Next, introduce students to a map of their own community. Discuss the location of various neighborhoods and your school.

Now, invite students to imagine that the town where the many characters of *Even Firefighters Hugs Their Moms* live and work is their town. As a group or individual activity, ask students to place each character from the story on their community map.

As a group, discuss why they chose each placement, asking students to support their choices using logic.

Language Arts Curriculum Connections

The Story Continues

After your students have completed the research and brainstorming of the What Do People Do All Day activity on p. 75, invite each group to use their graphic organizer to plan and write a sequel to *Even Firefighters Hug Their Moms* using the characters they have created.

First, invite them to analyze the structure and patterns in MacLean's book. They will find that each section follows this pattern:

- introduction of character by name and career title

- explanation of job responsibilities

- introduction of helper

- possible discussion of special clothing and equipment

- description of action

- Mom asks for a hug

- character explains why that is not possible

- Mom complains

Ask them to notice that there are added sounds, where appropriate, and quite a bit of humor.

Now, direct them to follow MacLean's pattern to create their own story.

Science Curriculum Connections

Science Goes to Work

Begin this activity by discussing the many fields of science, from medicine to aeronautics to engineering. Brainstorm as many branches of science as you can with students and discuss them to be sure that students have a clear understanding of what is studied in each. (You can find a list of the fields online at the Online Knowledge

Magazine MIStupid at www.mistupid.com/science/fields.htm.)

Then, ask whether students have noticed that each of the careers in *Even Firefighters Hug Their Moms* has a science connection. Some science connections are easy to see while others may require some thinking and discussion. Begin by taking a trip to the library media center to use nonfiction career and community helper books as well as print and online reference sources to learn what each worker does in his or her job.

Now, divide the class into groups. Assign four careers to each group. Invite groups to complete the Science Goes to Work graphic organizer on p. 80, listing the fields of science employed in each career. Lead a follow up discussion of how each branch of science comes into play.

Science Standards

Nature of Science

- Understands the scientific enterprise

What Do People Do All Day?

Character	Profession	Helper	Major Activities of the Character and His Helper						
Big Frank	Fire Fighter	Fire Fighter Sally							
Officer Dave	Police Officer	Rex (Police Dog)							
Joe	EMT	Junior							
Dan	Construction Worker	xx							
Captain Steve	Helicopter Pilot	xx							
Sam	Train Conductor	xx							
Neil	Astronaut	xx							
Rick	Garbage Truck Driver	xx							

Science Goes to Work
Graphic Organizer

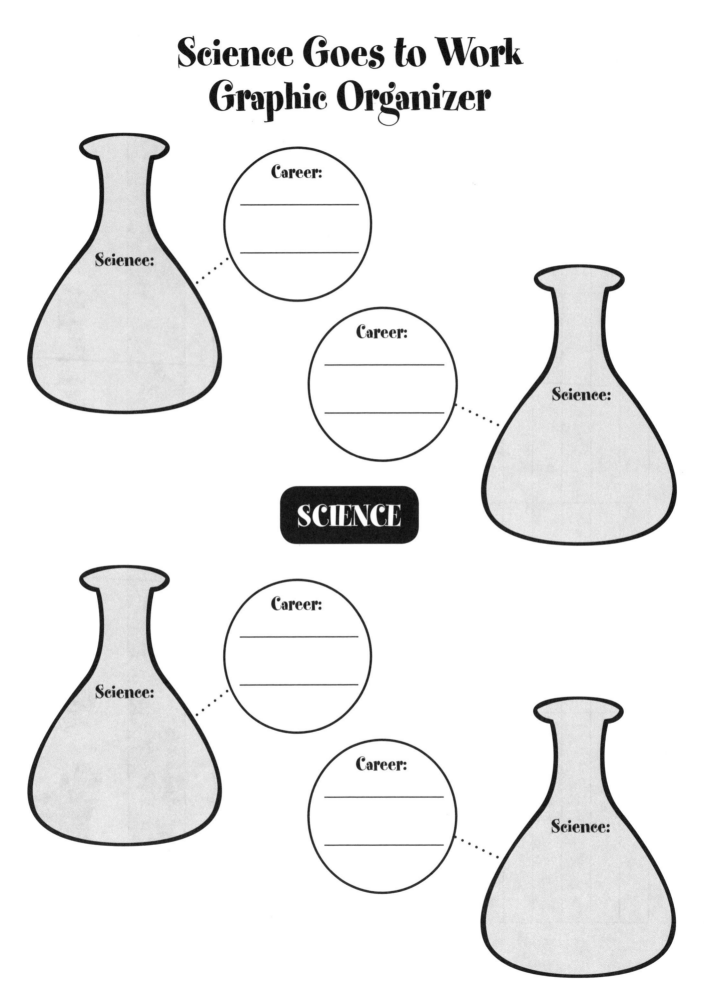

Career:
_____
_____

Science:

Career:
_____
_____

Science:

SCIENCE

Science:

Career:
_____
_____

Career:
_____
_____

Science:

Faraway Home

Read *Faraway Home* and the interview with Jane Kurtz below to familiarize yourself with the book and the author. Read the book aloud to children first, so that they can enjoy the illustrations and become familiar with the story. Then, hand out a set of photocopied scripts to eleven or thirteen students. (**Note:** Because Mother and Christopher each have a single line part, you may want to assign them to one of the two choruses as well.) Note that the America Chorus will include a chime player and the Africa Chorus will include a drummer. Your music teacher may be able to lend instruments for the reading. Ask the remaining children to be the audience. Have performers face the audience and simply read their parts on the first run-through. Once all readers are comfortable with their parts, have a second reading with the opportunity to use props, if desired, and to act out the story while reading.

Meet Jane Kurtz

Since 1990, Jane Kurtz has published twenty-three books: nonfiction books, professional books for teachers, picture books, and novels that draw on her own childhood memories of growing up in Ethiopia, on living through the Red River flood of 1997, on her great grandmother's adventures traveling the Oregon Trail, and on the minor crises of her children's lives—from struggles over wearing seat belts to not liking to get up in the morning. Her books have gathered accolades, starred reviews, and awards. A former elementary, secondary, and uni-

versity teacher, Jane is a frequent and popular visitor to schools around the world and is the co-founder of the first free library for children in Addis Ababa.

Please talk about your faraway home, Ethiopia.

JK: My parents moved to Ethiopia when I was only two years old, so in the early years of my life, I didn't have any memories of the United States where I'd been born. As I got older, I became aware that I was something

of an outsider in Ethiopia. In Maji, where I lived, my family, a nurse, and a teacher were the only people in my world who spoke English—or who had books. (My mom had read an article written by a librarian about one hundred best children's books, bought as many as she could afford, and packed them into the barrels for our birthdays and Christmas stockings.) During the two years when I visited the U.S., first as a seven-year-old and then as a thirteen-year-old, I felt even more of an outsider. By the time I was an adult, I had a hard time figuring out where "home" was for me.

Ironically, my life recently made a big, interesting circle. In 2003, I helped start the first free library for children in Addis Ababa, Ethiopia. My daughter, niece, and son went to volunteer at the library … and my son ended up getting married to a young Ethiopian woman working there. Now I have two Ethiopian-American grandbabies. Once I was like the father in *Faraway Home;* now it looks as if I might end up as the faraway grandmother, with sadness glimmering at the edges of my photographs.

In what ways does Desta's father's experience in *Faraway Home* mirror your own experience? How many of the visual images and situations are drawn from your personal history?

JK: By the time my own children were born, I'd decided I wanted to learn how to be an American, and—for me—that meant hardly ever discussing my years in Ethiopia. Writing eventually gave me a voice to talk about my childhood. When I was working on this picture book, I gave Desta's father my own memories. Although I didn't wrap myself in a cloak and sleep on the floor of my house, I grew up around children who

did, and I definitely did chew sugarcane and see hippos, crocodiles, waterfalls, rolling fog, and the cloud of flamingoes rippling the sky.

***Faraway Home* is dedicated to your daughter Rebekah "who always wanted to hear my stories about Ethiopia." Please tell us some of these stories so special to Rebekah.**

JK: Rebekah particularly liked me to talk about going off to boarding school in Addis Ababa when I was ten years old. She mostly wanted to hear the stories of times I got into trouble. For example, we were forbidden to play in the stone quarry where most of the materials for the school's buildings had been dug, but I couldn't stay away. One time, my friends and I returned from the quarry so muddy that we decided to break another rule and climb through the window to our room. Unfortunately, we left a muddy footprint on the windowsill. "What happened?" Rebekah would always ask. The same thing that happened if we talked and giggled after lights out: we could expect a knock and the words, "Girls, no dessert tomorrow." Actually, we usually told ourselves that it was probably tapioca ("fish eyes and glue") anyway, so we didn't mind.

Your book is also dedicated to "my Ethiopian friends whose real stories helped me write this book." How did their stories guide you to address the immigrant experience in this way?

JK: The specific true story that first gave me the idea for *Faraway Home* happened to Dr. Jerman Disasa, who grew up in Dembi Dollo, the town in southwest Ethiopia where the most talented students from Maji ended up going to high school. Jerman became a college professor in South

Carolina. When he showed a picture of himself to his children, his son stared at the picture and then asked, "Why did you take off your shoes to go to school?" As I was revising the story, it was a young Ethiopian-American mother (struggling with whether to return to Ethiopia to visit her own sick mother) who helped me find the conflict that became the heart of *Faraway Home's* plot.

What do you hope children know about the immigrant experience as a result of reading about Desta and her father?

JK: In the same way that writing finally gave me the voice to talk about my real childhood, I know writing has the power to give a voice to millions of children in classrooms in the United States. I hope *Faraway Home* will open opportunities for immigrant children to write about their real lives. I also hope my book will tweak some respectful curiosity for non-immigrant children about what it's like for a family to pick up life and move to a whole different country, leaving pieces behind. Finally, I hope my book makes everyone think for a few minutes about the universality of experiences. When I was doing a school visit in Grand Forks, North Dakota, one girl told me, "I know just how Desta feels—because I'm growing up in Grand Forks, and my dad grew up in Mandan." Mandan is only a few hours away from Grand Forks, but that girl had made an important connection.

Do any of your other books consider the immigrant experience? Tell us about them.

JK: *In the Small, Small Night* (Greenwillow Books, 2005) is the story of a brother and sister from Ghana who've recently landed in the United States. At night, the big sister tells stories of home to her little brother to help him remember, to keep them connected with their family at home, and to give them courage for their new life. *The Washington Post* named this book one of the best picture books of 2005. I also edited an acclaimed anthology of short stories, *Memories of Sun: Stories of Africa and America* (Greenwillow Books, 2004), with short stories for middle school and high school students. The book has three sections (Africa, Africans in America, and Americans in Africa), and the last section includes the true story of a young man from Eritrea who ended up graduating from Harvard, a story of a former child soldier, a story of an Americanized middle school girl thinking seriously about her family's history for the first time, and a story of one of the "Lost Boys" of the Sudan.

How can readers learn more about you and your books?

JK: I speak in schools and at conferences all over the U.S., so maybe some of your readers will meet me in person some day. A good way to meet the virtual me is to visit my Web site at www.janekurtz.com.

Where can young readers learn more about EBCEF? And are there ways that students can be involved in and contribute to EBCEF?

After my daughter returned to the U.S. following her volunteer experience in Ethiopia, she volunteered her time to design a Web site, www.ethiopiareads.org. Many students have done fundraisers to help keep EBCEF's first libraries and reading rooms open, and some have even written their own books to share with young readers in Ethiopia.

Books by Jane Kurtz

American Southwest Resource Book: The People, Vol. 1. Eakin Press, 1996.

Bicycle Madness. Henry Holt & Company, 2003.

Do Kangaroos Wear Seat Belts? Dutton, 2005.

Ethiopia: The Roof of Africa. Silver Burdett Press, 1991.

Faraway Home. Harcourt, 2000.

The Feverbird's Claw. Greenwillow Books, 2004.

Fire on the Mountain. Simon & Schuster, 1994.

I'm Sorry, Almira Ann. Henry Holt & Company, 1999.

In the Small, Small Night. Greenwillow Books, 2005.

Jakarta Missing. Greenwillow Books, 2001.

Johnny Appleseed. Aladdin, 2004.

Memories of Sun: Stories of Africa and America. Greenwillow Books, 2004.

Miro in the Kingdom of the Sun. Houghton Mifflin, 1996.

Mister Bones: Dinosaur Hunter. Aladdin Books, 2004.

Only a Pigeon. Simon & Schuster, 1997.

Oregon Trail: Chasing the Dream. Simon & Schuster, 2005.

Pulling the Lion's Tail. Simon & Schuster, 1995.

Rain Romp. Greenwillow Books, 2002.

River Friendly, River Wild. Simon & Schuster, 2000.

Saba: Under the Hyena's Foot. Pleasant Company Publications, 2003.

The Storyteller's Beads. Harcourt, 1998.

Terrific Connections with Authors, Illustrators and Storytellers: Real Space and Virtual Links with Toni Buzzeo. Libraries Unlimited, 1999.

35 Best Books for Teaching U.S. Regions with Toni Buzzeo. Scholastic Professional, 2002.

Treasury of the Southwest: Resources for Teachers and Students. Libraries Unlimited, 1992.

Trouble. Gulliver Books, 1997.

Water Hole Waiting. Greenwillow Books, 2002.

Faraway Home Script

Roles

Mother	Desta	Daddy	Christopher
Narrator One	Narrator Two	Narrator Three	

America Chorus (three readers, one with a chime)

Africa Chorus (three readers, one with a drum)

Pronunciation

These words are in Amharic. There are no stress syllables.

- **Injera:** in-jeh-rah

- **Gahbi:** gah-bee

- **Emayay:** em-eye-yay

Narrator One: When Desta dances into her house after school, the first thing she sees is the green envelope.

Narrator Two: She traces the bright stamp with her finger.

Mother: Your grandmother back home in Ethiopia is ill. Your father needs to go home to be with her.

Desta: Daddy is going to leave us? No!

Narrator Three: Desta runs to her father's favorite chair and curls up in it.

America Chorus: *(With chime.)* America, America, my right here home.

Narrator One: When evening comes, soft as a curtain closing, Desta's father takes her in his arms.

Daddy: Desta, my Desta, whose name means "joy," listen to my song.

Africa Chorus: *(With drum.)* Africa, Africa, my faraway home.

Narrator Two: Daddy sings a haunting song full of words Desta doesn't know.

Desta: Ethiopia is so far away. I don't want you to go.

Daddy:	For me, Ethiopia is never far away. Close your eyes and try to see green-gray mountains. Think about a thick cloud of fog crawling up the valley and the lonely sound of cowbells in the hills.
Africa Chorus:	*(With drum.)* Africa, Africa, my faraway home.
Narrator Three:	Desta closes her eyes and hears the wind chime hanging from the front porch.
Desta:	Do cowbells sound like that?
America Chorus:	*(With chime.)* America, America, my right here home.
Daddy:	When I was your age, I carried grain on my head to the mill by the waterfall, where the grain was ground into flour. Then my mother made *injera* and cooked it over the fire that lived in a scooped-out place in the middle of the floor.
Africa Chorus:	*(With drum.)* Africa, Africa, my faraway home.
Narrator One:	Desta shakes her head.
Narrator Two:	In her home the fire stays in a fireplace.
Narrator Three:	Her own mother cooks *injera* on the stove.
America Chorus:	*(With chime.)* America, America, my right here home.
Desta:	My friend Christopher says Africa is hot.
Narrator One:	Daddy clicks his tongue.
Daddy:	Not where I lived. Sometimes at night the wind whooshed cold as old bones through the silver blue leaves of the eucalyptus trees outside my home. I slept on the floor wrapped in my *gahbi* to keep warm.
Africa Chorus:	*(With drum.)* Africa, Africa, my faraway home.
Narrator Two:	Desta tries to imagine sleeping on the floor and listening to silver blue eucalyptus.
Narrator Three:	The tree she hears at night drops white blossoms on her bedroom windowsill, blossoms that look like snow.
America Chorus:	*(With chime.)* America, America, my right here home.
Daddy:	In Ethiopia, hippos yawn from muddy pools and crocodiles arch their backs above the river water. Shepherds pipe songs of longing in the hills, and thousands of flamingos

flap in a pink cloud over the Great Rift Valley lakes. I wish you could see the pink cloud.

Africa Chorus: *(With drum.)* Africa, Africa, my faraway home.

Desta: Did you walk to school like I do?

Daddy: Yes. And I carried a stick of purple sugarcane over my shoulder. Sometimes I couldn't wait for lunch but chewed out the sweet juices as I walked to school with mud squeezing up between my toes.

Africa Chorus: *(With drum.)* Africa, Africa, my faraway home.

Desta: Wait. Why did you take your shoes off?

Daddy: *(Laugh.)* I didn't wear shoes to school.

Desta: Didn't wear shoes?

Narrator Two: Desta thinks of the shoes in her closet—the black pair, the wonderful red pair, the new pair that she can hardly wait to wear.

Desta: No shoes. That's strange.

America Chorus: *(With chime.)* America, America, my right here home.

Narrator Three: Daddy gives Desta a mule ride to bed.

Narrator One: He switches on her night-light and takes her hand in his.

Daddy: Desta, my stomach is always hungry to go home. Now my *emayay* is very sick. It is time for me to go home and be with her for a while.

Africa Chorus: *(With drum.)* Africa, Africa, my faraway home.

Narrator Two: Desta thinks of hippos and crocodiles and a cold whooshing wind.

Desta: Daddy, would you like to take my night-light with you?

Daddy: Thank you, but my mother's home has no electricity. When I was a boy, sometimes the darkness pressed against me, and I heard the hyenas' strange coughing cry close by. But my *emayay* sang to me. She showed me that sunsets were bright borders on the cloth of the evening sky. The moon and stars burned holes in the cloth to light the night.

Africa Chorus: *(With drum.)* Africa, Africa, my faraway home.

Narrator Three: Desta looks out the window at the stars beyond the snow blossom tree.

Narrator One: She shivers to think of the hyenas' cry.

Desta: Don't leave us to go there. Your home is too wild.

Narrator Two: A sad look flies over Daddy's face, and before Desta goes to sleep, she hears him singing the haunting song with words she doesn't understand.

Desta: *(Whisper.)* Don't go. Don't go. Don't go.

America Chorus: *(With chime.)* America, America, my right here home.

Narrator Three: The next morning Desta walks to school, scuffing the toes of her shoes on the sidewalk.

Narrator One: The wind chime rings its rhymes all the way down her block.

Narrator Two: Desta wonders why Daddy has to remember things like cowbells and silver blue eucalyptus.

Desta: What if he goes away and never comes back?

America Chorus: *(With chime.)* America, America, my right here home.

Narrator One: Desta dreams all morning by the window. At lunch time, she sits with Christopher.

Desta: Did you ever hear of anyone not wearing shoes to school?

Christopher: No. That would be weird.

Narrator Two: Desta frowns. When Christopher leaves, she opens her locket and looks at the face of the grandmother she has never met but whose picture she wears close to her heart.

Narrator Three: Grandmother's eyes look back at her, proud and strong. But is there sadness glimmering in those eyes?

Narrator One: In the afternoon Desta looks up flamingos in the teacher's big book.

Narrator Two: As she studies their upside-down smiles, she thinks she almost hears the sound of a haunting lullaby somewhere at the edge of the classroom.

Africa Chorus: *(With drum.)* Africa, Africa, faraway home.

Narrator Three: After school Desta walks home barefoot, swinging her shoes, feeling the sun under her feet where it has soaked into the ground.

Africa Chorus: *(With drum.)* Africa, Africa, faraway home.

Narrator One: When evening comes, soft as a curtain closing, Desta climbs into her father's lap.

Desta: I think you miss your home a lot.

Daddy: Yes, I do.

Desta: *(Sigh.)* And your *emayay* misses you a lot.

Daddy: Yes. The same way I will miss you while I am gone.

Desta: Will you tell me about your home every night until you leave?

Narrator Two: Daddy holds Desta close.

Daddy: Oh yes. And when I come back—and I *will* come back—I will have new stories to tell.

Desta: Know what? Shoes aren't so great.

Narrator Three: Desta catches her father's smile and then closes her eyes.

Narrator One: Daddy will come back.

Narrator Two: Until he does, Desta can hold his stories in her heart.

Narrator Three: As Daddy sings to her, Desta sees a pink cloud of flamingos rippling up from a dark blue lake, wrinkling the pale cloth of the evening sky.

Africa Chorus: *(With drum.)* Africa, Africa, faraway home.

America Chorus: *(With chime.)* America, America, right here home.

Africa and America Choruses:
   (With drum and chime.) Africa, America, home.

The End

Social Studies Curriculum Connections

Africa is Not a Country

Many students have only a vague sense of the location of Africa and even less of an understanding of the great cultural and geographic diversity of the continent. To enhance their understanding of the location of Desta's Daddy's Africa home, introduce a map of the continent of Africa and begin by asking students to locate Ethiopia on the map. [**Note:** This is a perfect time to introduce atlases and teach atlas location skills.]

Now, ask students to brainstorm a list of facts they know about Ethiopia from reading *Faraway Home*. Require them to substantiate their claims by citing evidence in the text or illustrations of the book. Next, read a brief nonfiction book about Ethiopia to the class, such as *Ethiopia* by Noelle Morris (Raintree, 2004).

Ask students to add to their brainstormed list of facts about Ethiopia. Using these facts, ask them to fill in the All About Africa graphic organizer on p. 94. They can gather even more facts and information about Ethiopia at the PBS Africa: Explore the Regions pages on the Ethiopian Higlands at www.pbs.org/wnet/africa/explore/ethiopia/ethiopia_overview.html.

Finally, read the following book aloud:

- *Africa is Not a Country* by Margy Burns Knight and Mark Melnicove. Millbrook Press, 2000.

Lead a discussion of the ways that Ethiopia is different from other African countries they encounter in this book.

> **Geography Standards**
>
> **The World in Spatial Terms**
>
> - Understands the characteristics and uses of maps, globes, and other geographic tools and technologies
>
> - Knows the location of places, geographic features, and patterns of the environment
>
> **Reading Standards**
>
> - Uses reading skills and strategies to understand and interpret a variety of informational texts

All About Africa

After you have completed the Africa is Not a Country activity (at left), supply all students with a blackline map of Africa (available online at abcteach® at www.abcteach.com/Maps/images/africa48.gif). Ask them to begin by coloring in Ethiopia. Next, divide the class into seven groups of students. Assign each group a region of the continent:

- Sahara
- Sahel
- Savanna
- Swahili Coast
- Rainforest
- Great Lakes
- Southern Africa

PBS has an excellent guide to the regions of Africa at www.pbs.org/wnet/africa/explore/index_flash.html.

Ask each group to select a country in their assigned region, locate their country on a map of the African continent, and color it in on their blackline map as well. Now, invite each group to conduct research on one country from their region in the library media center and complete the All About Africa graphic organizer on p. 94.

Many Places to Visit

When each group has completed its All About Africa graphic organizer, create a classroom matrix on a white board or chart paper on the wall. List countries vertically and the eight fact categories across the top. Ask groups to fill in the information for their selected country from their research.

Now, host a class discussion about the similarities and differences between the various African countries researched. Invite students to share visual images from their research as well. At the end of the discussion, invite each student to decide where he or she would most like to visit and ask him or her to tell the class why.

Who Lives in Our Community?

Most communities in America include people who are either first-generation immigrants to the United States, like Desta's father, or whose ancestors came to this country from other parts of the world. Beginning in your own classroom, invite students to explore their family heritage. (Of course, it is important to be sensitive to the fact that some students may be living in dual cultures or outside their biologically hereditary culture as a result of adoption, intermarriage, or complex family patterns.)

Create a Who Lives in Our Community? world map display (see sample on p. 95) in the hall, marking the country of origin and approximate year the family first arrived in the United States for any student who is able to provide this information. If families would like to share photographs, these may encircle the map and be attached by yarn to the pushpin in the country of origin on the map. Invite students to survey teachers and students in other classes to determine their family's countries of origin and add them to the display.

Finally, if it is possible through a cultural heritage center in your community, offer students the opportunity to interview and visit with recent immigrants to the United States. The goal of this activity is to celebrate a diversity of cultures in your community.

Science Curriculum Connections

Animals of Ethiopia

Daddy tells Desta about the hippos, crocodiles, hyenas, and flamingoes of his African home in Ethiopia when he was growing up. These animals and more are an important way in which Ethiopia is different from your community. Invite students to research the animals of Ethiopia. You might consider including:

- blue-winged goose*
- crocodile
- Ethiopian wolf*
- flamingo
- gelada baboon*
- hippopotamus
- hyena
- mountain nyala*
- walia ibex*
- wattled ibis*

* Information may be found at www.pbs.org/wnet/africa/explore/ethiopia/ethiopia_animals.html

Especially good resources for this research are:

- *eNature.* www.enature.com.
- *Wildlife and Plants of the World.* Marshall Cavendish, 1999.

Use the Animals of Ethiopia graphic organizer on p. 96 to record the results of student research. Ask students to explain how each animal is especially adapted to its environment.

Language Arts Curriculum Connections

Remembering a Special Place

It is important to Desta's Daddy that he shares his memories of his mountain home with his daughter. He paints a picture of Ethiopia for her using the five senses. For example:

- he sings a haunting song in another language

- he describes the thick cloud of fog crawling up the valley

- he remembers the lonely sound of cowbells in the hills

Ask students to list all of the ways in which he paints a picture for Desta and identify the sense that he is using for each.

Now, invite students to choose a special place of their own. Ask them to create a list of the things they would describe to someone who had never been there. Challenge them to write at least one item for each of the five senses, more if possible.

Ask students to create individual poems from the lines of description they have written about their special places.

Language Arts Standards

Reading Standards

- Uses reading skills and strategies to understand and interpret a variety of literary texts

Writing Standards

- Uses the stylistic and rhetorical aspects of writing

All About Africa Graphic Organizer

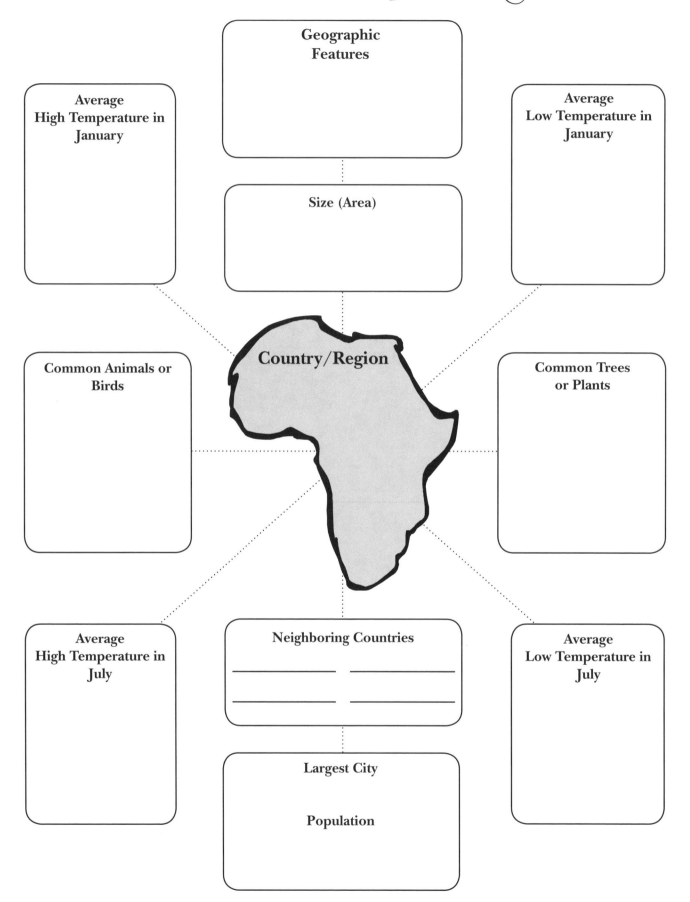

Geographic Features

Average High Temperature in January

Average Low Temperature in January

Size (Area)

Country/Region

Common Animals or Birds

Common Trees or Plants

Average High Temperature in July

Neighboring Countries

_____   _____

_____   _____

Average Low Temperature in July

Largest City

Population

Who Lives in Our Community?
Sample Bulletin Board

Animals of Ethiopia

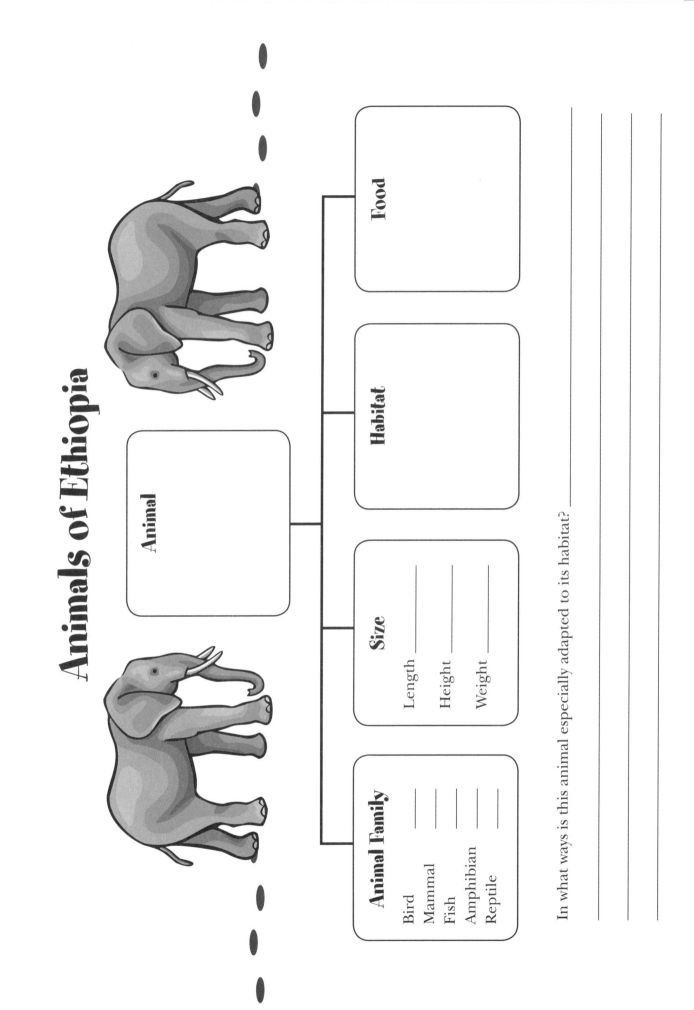

Animal

Animal Family

Bird
Mammal
Fish
Amphibian
Reptile

Size

Length _____
Height _____
Weight _____

Habitat

Food

In what ways is this animal especially adapted to its habitat? _____

_____

_____

Freedom Summer

Read *Freedom Summer* and the interview with Deborah Wiles to familiarize yourself with the book and the author. Read the book aloud to children first, so that they can enjoy the illustrations and become familiar with the story. Then, hand out a set of photocopied scripts to ten children. (**Note:** The parts of Mr. Mason, Daddy, Mama, and especially Boss Man are brief and perfect for challenged readers who need to gain confidence with oral reading.) Ask the remaining children to be the audience. Give readers time to practice their reading until they are fluent. Have performers face the audience and simply read their parts on the first run-through. Once all readers are comfortable with their parts, have a second reading with the opportunity to use costumes or props if desired, and to act out the story while reading.

Meet Deborah Wiles

Deborah Wiles was born in Alabama into an Air Force family and spent her growing-up summers in a small Mississippi town with an extended family full of Southern characters. Today she writes about them and they live on in her stories. Her work has received the Ezra Jack Keats New Writer Award, the PEN/Phyllis Reynolds Naylor Working Writer Fellowship, and a Golden Kite Honor from SCBWI. Her recent novel, *Each Little Bird That Sings,* was awarded the E. B. White Read Aloud Award, and was a 2005 National Book Award finalist. Deborah lives in Atlanta, Georgia, where she avoids the traffic, climbs Stone Mountain, and grows the world's most beautiful zinnias.

Your "A Note about the Text" in *Freedom Summer,* gives us a glimpse into how you came to write this story. Please talk more about growing up in the South of the fifties and sixties and its influence on this story.

DW: We moved whenever my father was transferred in the military, but we spent summers in Mississippi at my father's childhood home. I loved the place and the people with all my heart. I felt loved unconditionally in Mississippi, by a cast of real characters who told outlandish southern stories that I knew must be true. In

that insular world, I never noticed a hint of racism. Then the town pool closed, the ice cream parlor closed, and I began asking questions, began watching the news, began paying attention, and my world changed. Mississippi is a land of contradictions. Those contradictions—great love, great hate—form the basis for *Freedom Summer*. Joe and John Henry are best friends, and they love one another in the way I was loved during those summers in Mississippi. They end up making a life-changing decision for themselves and one another.

There is a strong sense of place in your book. How many of the visual images and sensory details of the story are drawn from your personal history? What are your memories?

DW: Mississippi was a feast for my senses ... it was a world apart from any other I knew— and I lived all over the globe. I remember so well the feel of the butterbeans I shelled on the porch with my great-grandmother, the taste of sweet iced tea and fried okra, the smell of a hot summer afternoon and my sweat rolling down my nose, I remember how wonderful that dark-blue water felt as I plunged into Lake Walkaway, and the sound of the locusts rising and falling in that old chorus, the way the moths danced around the porch light at night—all of these details find their way into *Freedom Summer*.

Do others of your books also consider the racial strife in the South or reflect your childhood experiences growing up in the region?

DW: Most of my fiction is centered in the deep South and is full of its eccentricities, right down to the names I give my characters. I created white worlds in my first two novels, as that was the only world I knew at

first. In the novels I'm working on now, I'm creating a racially diverse South. I'm following in fiction the progression I lived as a child, moving from a Mississippi where I had relationships with only white people, to a world that encompasses lots of racial diversity and its accompanying joys and difficulties. I'm finding it rich and rewarding work; I'm hoping I do these stories justice. That's what I tried to do in *Freedom Summer*.

***Freedom Summer* is dedicated to "the children of the movement" in part. Please share your feelings about these children and what the civil rights movement meant to them, to us.**

DW: I can't speak about what the civil rights movement meant to anyone but me, and what it meant to me was that I had an awakening. It was the beginning of a true sense of empathy for me (and it came at an age-appropriate time, the year I turned 11), of wondering what it would be like to be someone else—a child, particularly—in a situation that was different from mine socially, culturally, racially. What would it be like to be treated so unfairly? And what could I do about that? What could anyone do? Did we have power? Could we claim it? How? These are issues I struggle with today, as well.

What do you hope children know about the Civil Rights Act and its meaning for individuals in the sixties as a result of reading about Young Joe and John Henry?

DW: I'd love for children to read *Freedom Summer* as a story about friendship, justice, and empowerment. In schools I always point out that 100 years passed between the abolishment of slavery in this country and the passage of the Civil Rights Act, which is something that children often don't realize, that they have parents and grandparents

living today who witnessed and who may have participated in the struggle for civil rights. The passage of time is a hard concept to teach, even to adults sometimes. The concept of justice-for-all, the formation of character, and the consequences of choice—these are ideas I wanted to explore in *Freedom Summer* and would love for teachers to explore with students, for children to explore with one another.

You are well known as a middle grade novelist, yet *Freedom Summer* is a picture book. What is exciting, interesting, rewarding, and/or challenging about writing in this shorter format?

DW: It's hard to write short! And within this shorter form, it's crucial to develop characters and stories with depth and heart—I love this challenge. I think of *Freedom Summer* as a prose poem, which is how it was written.

How can readers learn more about you and your books?

DW: They can visit my Web site at www.deborahwiles.com.

Books by Deborah Wiles

Aurora County All-Stars. Harcourt, 2007.

each little bird that sings. Harcourt, 2005.

Freedom Summer. Simon & Schuster, 2001.

Love, Ruby Lavender. Harcourt, 2001.

One Wide Sky: A Bedtime Lullaby. Harcourt, 2003.

A Note about the Text from Freedom Summer

In the early 1960s the American South had long been a place where black Americans could not drink from the same drinking fountains as whites, attend the same schools, or enjoy the same public areas. Then the Civil Rights Act of 1964 became law and stated that "All persons shall be entitled to the full and equal enjoyment" of any public place, regardless of "... race, color, religion, or national origin."

I was born a white child in Mobile, Alabama, and spent summers visiting my beloved Mississippi relatives. When the Civil Rights Act was passed, the town pool closed. So did the roller rink and ice cream parlor. Rather than lawfully giving blacks the same rights and freedoms as whites, many southern businesses chose to shut their doors in protest. Some of them closed forever.

Also in the summer of 1964, civil rights workers in Mississippi organized "Freedom Summer," a movement to register black Americans to vote. It was a time of great racial violence and change. That was the summer I began to pay attention: I noticed that black Americans used back doors, were waited on only after every white had been helped, and were treated poorly, all because of the color of their skin ... and no matter what any law said. I realized that a white person openly having a black friend, and vice versa, could be a dangerous thing. I couldn't get these thoughts and images out of my mind, and I wondered what it must be like to be a black child my age. I dreamed about changing things, and yet I wondered what any child—black or white—could do.

This story grew out of my feelings surrounding that time. It is fiction, but based on real events.

Freedom Summer Script

Young Joe: John Henry Waddell is my best friend. His mama, Annie Mae, works for my mama.

Annie Mae: Every morning at eight o'clock I step off the county bus and walk up the long hill to Young Joe's house.

John Henry: If it's summer, I'm step-step-stepping-it right beside my mama.

Young Joe: We like to help Annie Mae.

John Henry: We shell butter beans.

Young Joe: We sweep the front porch.

John Henry: We let the cats in, and chase the cats out of the house until Mama sends us out.

Annie Mae: Shoo! Enough of you two! Go play!

Young Joe: We shoot marbles in the dirt until we're too hot to be alive.

John Henry: Then we run straight for Fiddler's Creek.

Young Joe and John Henry:
(Yell.) Last one in is a rotten egg!

Young Joe: John Henry swims better than anyone I know.

John Henry: I crawl like a catfish, blow bubbles like a swamp monster.

Young Joe: But he doesn't swim in the town pool with me.

Chorus: He's not allowed.

Young Joe and John Henry:
So we dam the creek with rocks and sticks to make a swimming spot, then holler and jump in, wearing only our skin.

Young Joe: John Henry's skin is the color of brown butter. He smells like pine needles after a good rain. My skin is the color of the pale moths that dance around the porch late at night.

John Henry: You smell like a just-washed sock.

Young Joe: *(Shout.)* This means war!

Young Joe and John Henry:

We churn that water into a white hurricane and laugh until our sides hurt. Then we float on our backs and spout like whales.

Young Joe: I'm going to be a fireman when I grow up.

John Henry: Me, too.

Young Joe: I have two nickels for ice pops, so we put on our clothes and walk to town.

John Henry: I don't go through the front door of Mr. Mason's General Store with Young Joe.

Chorus: He's not allowed.

Mr. Mason: How you doin', Young Joe?

Chorus: Mr. Mason winks.

Mr. Mason: You gonna eat these all by yourself?

Young Joe: I got one for a friend.

Mr. Mason: Yessir, it's mighty hot out there!

Young Joe: My heart does a quick-beat and I scoot out the door.

John Henry: I love ice pops.

Young Joe: Me, too.

Annie Mae: I make dinner for Young Joe's family every night.

Young Joe: She creams the corn and rolls the biscuits. Daddy stirs the iced tea.

Daddy: The town pool opens tomorrow to everybody under the sun, no matter what color.

Mama: That's the new law.

Young Joe: She heaps my plate with peas.

Mama: It's the way it's going to be now.

Young Joe:	I wiggle in my chair like a doodlebug.
Mama:	Everybody Together—lunch counters, rest rooms, drinking fountains, too.
Young Joe:	*(Shout.)* I got to be excused!
John Henry:	Young Joe runs into the kitchen.
Young Joe:	The town pool opens tomorrow to everybody under the sun, no matter what color. Mama says that's the new law!
John Henry:	*(Holler.)* I'm gonna swim in the town pool! Is it deep?
Young Joe:	REAL deep. And the water's so clear, you can jump to the bottom and open your eyes and still see.
John Henry:	Let's be the first ones there. I'll bring my good-luck nickel, and we can dive for it.
Young Joe:	Next morning, as soon as the sun peeks into the sky, here comes my best friend, John Henry Waddell, run-run-running to meet me.
John Henry:	*(Yell.)* Let's go! I got my nickel.
Young Joe:	I run right with him, all the way to the town swimming pool.
Young Joe and John Henry:	We race each other over the last hill and …
Chorus:	They stop.
John Henry:	County dump trucks are here.
Young Joe:	They grind and back up to the empty pool.
John Henry:	Workers rake steaming asphalt into the hole where sparkling clean water used to be.
Young Joe:	One of them is John Henry's big brother, Will Rogers.
Young Joe and John Henry:	*(Call.)* What's happened?
John Henry:	He sees us and points back on down the road—
Chorus:	It means 'Git on home!'
John Henry:	But we feel stuck, we can't budge.
Young Joe:	So we hunker in the tall weeds and watch all morning until the pool is filled with hot, spongy tar.

Chorus:	Sssssss! Smoky steam rises in the air.
Young Joe:	Workers tie planks to their shoes and stomp on the blacktop to make it smooth.
John Henry:	My brother heaves his shovel into the back of an empty truck and climbs up with the other workers.
Young Joe:	His face is like a storm cloud, and I know this job has made him angry.
Boss Man:	*(Shout.)* Let's go!
John Henry:	The trucks rumble-slam down the road.
Chorus:	It is so quiet now, they can hear the breeze whisper through the grass.
Young Joe and John Henry:	
	We sit on the diving board and stare at the tops of the silver ladders sticking up from the tar.
Young Joe:	My heart beats hard in my chest. John Henry's voice shakes.
John Henry:	White folks don't want colored folks in their pool.
Young Joe:	You're wrong, John Henry.
Chorus:	But John Henry is right.
Young Joe:	Let's go back to Fiddler's Creek. I didn't want to swim in this old pool anyway.
Chorus:	John Henry's eyes fill up with angry tears.
John Henry:	I did. I wanted to swim in this pool. I wanted to do everything you can do.
Young Joe:	I don't know what to say.
John Henry:	We walk back to town.
Young Joe:	My head starts to pop with new ideas. I want to go to the Dairy Dip with John Henry, sit down, and share a root beer float. I want us to go to the picture show, buy popcorn, and watch the movie together. I want to see this town with John Henry's eyes.
John Henry:	We stop in front of Mr. Mason's store.

Young Joe: I jam my hands into my pockets while my mind searches for words to put with my new ideas.

John Henry: Young Joe pulls out two nickels.

Young Joe: Want to get an ice pop?

Chorus: John Henry wipes his eyes and takes a breath.

John Henry: I want to pick it out myself.

Chorus: Young Joe's heart says yes.

John Henry: I wait while Young Joe swallows hard.

Young Joe: Let's do that.

John Henry: Young Joe gives me one of his nickels.

Chorus: John Henry shakes his head.

John Henry: I got my own.

Chorus: They look at each other.

Young Joe and John Henry:
Then we walk through the front door together.

The End

Freedom Summer Activities

Language Arts Curriculum Connections

Seeing with New Eyes

Many times, it is difficult for students to understand historical events, coming as they do from a modern perspective. Thus, it's important to create an historical context for them from which they can consider, discuss, and respond to the events they encounter in the fiction they read.

After sharing *Freedom Summer* with students, begin to broaden their understanding by reading a poetic overview of the civil rights movement in *This is the Dream* by Diane Z. Shore and Jessica Alexander (HarperCollins, 2006).

Then read other picture books about race relations in the civil rights era, including:

- *Freedom School, Yes!* by Amy Littlesugar. Philomel, 2001.

- *The Other Side* by Jacqueline Woodson. Putnam, 2001.

- *White Socks Only* by Evelyn Coleman. Albert Whitman, 1996.

Invite students to discuss the personal friendships, race relations, and feelings of the characters in each of the additional picture books. Ask each student which character from the four picture books, including *Freedom Summer,* he or she is most drawn to and why.

What Would You Do?

Re-read "A Note About the Text" from *Freedom Summer* on p. 99 to remind students of the history of that time. Then invite students to select one of the characters in the book:

- Young Joe

- John Henry

- Annie Mae

- Mr. Mason

- Daddy

- Mama

- Will Rogers

Ask them to write about the summer of 1964, "Freedom Summer," in the voice of that character, discussing what has happened with the passage of the Civil Rights Act of 1964 and how they feel about it. Is the change a positive one? A dangerous one? A hopeful one? How does that character plan to respond to the changes?

Round Table Discussions

Once students have finished writing a piece from their chosen character's perspective in What Would You Do? on p. 105, stage a series of "round table discussions" in which students, representing each of the characters, meet at a table to answer your questions and represent their thinking about the changes the Civil Rights Act has brought.

Consider asking them the following questions:

- Is racial segregation a good or bad idea? Why?

- Should black and white children attend the same or different schools? Why?

- Would you or would you not participate in a civil rights march? Why?

- What do you think about Freedom Schools? Why do you think this?

Remind students that they should not express their own beliefs but remain in character.

Music Curriculum Connections

Protest songs were one of the avenues for solidarity and expression in the civil rights movement. From songs new in the sixties to traditional songs sung anew in the fight for equal rights for the races, the lyrics of these songs have power.

Ask students to read the lyrics and listen to the music of these civil rights songs. Then, as a group, discuss their meaning in the context of the civil rights movement.

Oh Freedom

Lyrics: www.negrospirituals.com/news-song/oh_freedom.htm

Music File: available for purchase ($0.99) at iTunes, www.apple.com/itunes/store/

We Shall Overcome/ Peter, Paul & Mary

Lyrics: www.peterpaulandmary.com/music/f-17-13.htm

Music File: available for purchase ($0.99) at iTunes, www.apple.com/itunes/store/

Blowin' in the Wind/Bob Dylan

Lyrics: bobdylan.com/songs/blowin.html

Music File: bobdylan.com/albums/freewheelin.html

We Shall Not Be Moved/Rutha Harris

Lyrics: humanitiesinstitute.utexas.edu/resources/toolkit/music/lyrics/We_Shall_Not.pdf

Music File: available for purchase ($0.99) at iTunes, www.apple.com/itunes/store/

This Little Light of Mine

Lyrics: www.songsforteaching.com/billharley/thislittlelightofmine.htm

Music File: available for purchase ($0.99) at iTunes, www.apple.com/itunes/store/

If you are searching for a collection of civil rights music for children, consider:

- *I'm Gonna Let It Shine: A Gathering of Voices for Freedom* by Bill Harley. Round River, 1990.

Arts Standards

Music Standards

- Understands the relationship between music and history and culture

---

Social Studies Curriculum Standards

Travel Back to Freedom Summer

Many times, images tell much more of a story than words (or words alone) can tell. This is certainly true in *Freedom Summer*. Begin by discussing the role of the illustrations in Deborah Wiles's picture book. Ask students what information we get from the pictures alone. Do we learn more about the events of the story, about the characters and their feelings?

Following this discussion, select images from the many available at the Veterans of the Civil Rights Movement Web site, particularly those in the "Freedom Summer" collection. Share them with your students. (**Note:** Keep in mind the violence of the time and choose carefully those images that will speak powerfully to children without frightening them.)

Ask students to choose a single photograph. Using the Travel Back to Freedom Summer graphic organizer on p. 108, ask them to write a personal reflection on the photograph and it's meaning to them as a result of all they have learned in this unit.

History Standards

Grades K–4: Topic 3—The History of the United States: Democratic Principles and Values and the People from Many Cultures who Contributed to its Cultural, Economic, and Political Heritage

- Understands how democratic values came to be, and how they have been exemplified by people, events, and symbols

Language Arts Standards

Writing Standards

- Uses the stylistic and rhetorical aspects of writing

Listening and Speaking

- Uses listening and speaking strategies for different purposes

Travel Back to Freedom Summer

_____

_____

_____

_____

_____

_____

_____

_____

Monsoon

Read *Monsoon* and the interview with Uma Krishnaswami to familiarize yourself with the book and the author. Read the book aloud to children first, so that they can enjoy the illustrations and become familiar with the story. Then, hand out a set of photocopied scripts to ten children. Ask the remaining children to be the audience. Or, because the chorus parts in this Reader's Theater lend themselves well to large group reading, choose readers for the seven designated reading parts and invite the remainder of the students to be the chorus. Have performers face the audience and simply read their parts on the first run-through. Once all readers are comfortable with their parts, have a second reading with the opportunity to use costumes or props if desired, and to act out the story while reading.

Meet Uma Krishnaswami

Uma Krishnaswami was born in India. She grew up hearing stories from Indian traditions, and reading children's books by British authors. As a child, she often escaped to a banyan tree to read undisturbed. As a result, for quite a long time she was convinced that Pooh's Hundred Acre Wood had banyan trees in it. Uma is the author of several picture books for children including *Monsoon, The Happiest Tree: A Yoga Story,* and *The Closet Ghosts.* She also teaches writing by invitation in schools and communities nationwide, and online through writers.com. Uma is married, with one son and two cats.

You were born in India, the setting for *Monsoon*. Please talk about the land of your birth and its influence on your writing.

UK: I think that in some ways we all filter our thinking through our personal geographies. India is part of my molecules so it finds expression in my writing. It's that simple. That's not to say I would never write a story without an Indian context, but I have felt driven for years to write about those connections that are uniquely mine.

Mind you, it's not just nostalgia. That gets knocked out of me pretty fast every time I visit India, given how much changes between my visits. And it's not that I feel I'm some kind of cultural representative. I've moved around enough in my life that sometimes I feel I'm a culture of one. It's just that there are a lot of stories hiding in the nooks and crannies of all writers' experiences. It happens that the subcontinent is very much a part of mine.

What was the origin of *Monsoon* for you? How many of the delicious images were drawn from real-life experiences?

UK: Many of them. My mother's youngest sister lived with us for awhile when we lived in Delhi in the 1960s. She was 14 years younger than my mother and 14 years older than me, and she treated me like an honorary sibling. She taught me to fold paper boats and I would launch flotillas on the first monsoon puddles in the garden. We didn't have TV, so I made that part up because a child today would certainly see the news as well as hear it. I did play hopscotch on the "pavement" (sidewalk) outside our house—with the neighbors' kids, as I didn't have a brother.

Monsoon began as a 12-line poem. I wrote it to calm my nerves while in a plane that was queued to land at Delhi airport just as a rainstorm was breaking out. It had heat waves rising off rocks, a peacock, and that songbird with a voice like liquid sunshine. It had no child character, no progression of narrative. It was what it was. It kept recurring in my writing journal—by the time a year had passed, I'd written and expanded it half a dozen times. Then I took it to my writers' group and they said, "It feels empty.

Where are the people?" In the next round, the girl walked into the story and she really shaped the rest of its growth.

In what ways is the young girl in *Monsoon* like you as a child? Were you a worrier? Were you a skeptic?

UK: I was a worrier, but I think I was a believer rather than a skeptic. If you told me that jumping a certain way would make it rain, I'd jump. The child in *Monsoon* is also far more coordinated than I was— that's [the illustrator] Jamel Akib's doing; I can't take credit for it. I was a clumsy child, with perpetually skinned knees, hair out of place, clothes a mess. There wasn't enough time for those things in my life. I was far too busy trying to make sense of the world!

***Monsoon* is a story of the emotional journey of a child and the people around her as dictated by the weather. Please talk about your personal connection to the weather and landscape in the places you have lived.**

UK: I live in northwest New Mexico now, and in this region, too, we wait for rain with bated breath. Right now, the wind is blowing fiercely outside, whirling dust up in great clouds so we've had to rush around and close all the windows. We joke here that every spring Arizona picks up and blows through New Mexico. Today it's threatening to take some tree limbs with it.

Weather and landforms are so powerful. The rocky landscapes around me in New Mexico, and a great variety of landscapes in India but most of all the mountains, have something in common. To the people of both regions, the land is traditionally held to be sacred. That's present in all the stories that interpret the land in terms of mythic

events—here it's First People and eagles, bears and coyotes, and twins, there it's lions, monkeys and bears, a river as a goddess, a whole mountain as an herbarium. And the earth is always Mother. In essence most ancient traditions are telling us to tread gently on this mother's body, only we've stopped listening. A couple of years ago I wrote a poem, "Lifeline," that deals with this connection I feel to the physicality of the only world we have. It was published in *Cicada* in July/August 2005.

What are some of the many things you hope that children will understand about South Asia after reading your story?

UK: That this is one facet of the region. The slice of South Asia shown in *Monsoon* is urban and bustling and exists in the present, with traffic jams and cybercafes. I wanted to offer a picture different from the India of *Jungle Book*. I want children to understand from this that real children live in the countries of South Asia and relate to each other and to adults and to the places they live in. I wanted to depict a place that was particular and textured, and characters experiencing something very universal in that place—a seasonal change.

How can readers learn more about you and your books?

UK: I have a Web site, www.umakrishnaswami.com, that I try to keep current. My son used to be my Webmaster, but now he's off in college so I've had to become more technically self-reliant. Check the Web site for updates on my books and other writing and teaching projects.

Books by Uma Krishnaswami

Ants Have a Picnic. Benchmark Education, 2006.

Big Party. Benchmark Education, 2006.

Bringing Asha Home. Lee & Low Books, 2006.

The Broken Tusk. Linnet Books, 1996.

Chachaji's Cup. Children's Book Press, 2003.

The Closet Ghosts. Children's Book Press, 2006.

The Happiest Tree: A Yoga Story. Lee & Low Books, 2005.

Holi. Children's Press, 2003.

Hooray 100 Days. Benchmark Education, 2006.

Learn to Estimate. Benchmark Education, 2006.

Monsoon. Farrar, Straus and Giroux, 2003.

Naming Maya. Farrar, Straus and Giroux, 2004.

Remembering Grandpa. Boyds Mills Press, 2007.

Stories of the Flood. Roberts Rinehard, 1994.

Monsoon Script

Roles

Main Character	Papa	Mummy	Nani
Brother	Narrator One	Narrator Two	
Chorus (three readers)			

Main Character: All summer we have worn the scent of dust—gravelly, grainy, gritty dust—blowing on the winds and sprinkling through our clothes and hair.

Narrator One: Even at breakfast, the dust is all we talk about.

Papa: When the monsoon rains arrive they'll wash this dust away.

Main Character: Going to the market, I cross the road with Mummy.

Mummy: We need tomatoes and maybe some beans.

Main Character: We pass the old tea stall. It clatters with the chink of cups, hums and thrums with wondering and worrying.

Chorus: Will monsoon rains come soon?

Narrator Two: The radio crackles with news of rain showers by the sea.

Main Character: But that seashore is far from us. Mummy sighs. She watches the sky, and she has questions.

Mummy: How much will it rain? How fast, how hard?

Main Character: She worries about floods, and so I worry too.

Narrator One: And there is another question.

Narrator Two: No one dares to ask it.

Main Character: It hangs in my mind, as the cry of the crows in the old neem tree hangs in the dust-pink air.

Chorus: What if they never come, those monsoon rains?

Main Character: Still in the afternoon, as Mummy chops and stirs and lunch smells fill the air, my busy hands fold paper boats. I crease their crisp white sails. In my mind I see them float in oceans of puddles.

Narrator One: Evening falls.

Main Character: I watch the faces on TV. Old and young, poor and rich, all across India, we wait for rain. The heat makes me feel like a crocodile crouching snap-jawed.

Narrator Two: Papa comes from work.

Main Character: I run down to meet him.

Narrator One: Across the street people crowd around the bus-stop shelter.

Main Character: Between the screeching of brakes and the scrambling of feet, I hear excitement.

Chorus: Wait! Listen! Was that thunder or the rumble of an engine?

Main Character: At bedtime, Nani tells us tales.

Nani: I remember how the monsoon was wetter, fuller, longer, back in the days before fields gave way to city streets.

Main Character: I listen, till her stories fade to dreams. Before day breaks, I hear a koel sing long and wild, in a voice like melting sunshine.

Chorus: Koooweeeel. Koooweeeel. Koooweeeel.

Narrator Two: From faraway a peacock wails.

Chorus: Ayoww! Ayoww! Ayoww!

Main Character: Ayoww! Ayoww! Ayoww! I answer him out loud, and startle everyone awake.

Narrator One: Hot loo winds tear through the city.

Narrator Two: They rip the paper off billboards and shred the smiles of movie stars.

Main Character: I complain, but Papa smiles.

Papa: We need this hot, dry wind to ripen those sweet mangoes.

Narrator One: Waves of heat dance upon rocks and shimmer over rooftops.

Narrator Two: But by the afternoon, long gray clouds begin to trail across the sky.

Nani: You'll see. When those partridge-feather clouds arrive, the monsoon rain will follow.

Main Character: Can we go play?

Narrator One: Nani looks up at the sky.

Nani: Don't take too long.

Main Character: In the hopscotch square we've chalked in the alley, my brother and I jump and hop and whirl to the sound of temple bells.

Chorus: Clanging. Clanging.

Brother: Three forward and three back and no stops in between will make it rain.

Main Character: That's silly.

Narrator Two: She tries it anyway.

Narrator One: In the street, a taxi driver honks an angry horn, but the old cow is tired and will not move.

Narrator Two: Wheels inch around her.

Main Character and Brother:
(*Laugh.*) The driver frowns and wags his head at us, and tears off in a cloud of dust.

Main Character: As we head home, the sky is filled with full, fat clouds.

Narrator One: The wispy feather trails are gone.

Narrator Two: From far away, thunder pounds a giant heartbeat.

Main Character and Brother:
We know. It won't be long.

Narrator One: The wind ruffles the leaves on the old neem tree.

Narrator Two: The newspaper man swishes plastic bags over the day's headlines.

Narrator One: Suddenly, it is still, a stillness filled with the scent of ripe mangoes …

Narrator Two: … with promises of dampness in the air.

Main Character: Then—oh!—the rain, the perfect rain, the stretching, sweeping sheet of rain storms down.

Narrator One:	Umbrellas turn into walking forests.
Main Character:	I sigh, and my sigh rides up to the sky. The raindrops make me laugh out loud, thudding on earth and rooftops and on my skin.
Narrator Two:	Mummy and Nani cross the street to clink a coin at the feet of potbellied Ganesh, god of beginnings.
Narrators One and Two:	
	Rivers gush along yesterday's roads.
Main Character:	I dance with the joy of earth's sudden sweet scent.

The End

A Note from Uma Krishnaswami: About the Monsoon

The word "monsoon" comes from an old Arabic word, *mausim*, meaning "season." The monsoon is the season of rain.

For a monsoon to happen, you need blisteringly hot land. Heated air rising off the earth's surface makes room for strong, wet winds to sweep in from the ocean. The winds in South and Southeast Asia blow from the northeast in winter and the southwest in summer. When they pass over the Indian Ocean and the Arabian Sea, they pick up moisture, and get wetter and wetter. Clouds form and are whirled along. Sometimes migrating birds catch a ride, too. The earth's rotation causes the winds to "bend" in giant swirls. Where mountains and landforms block the water-laden winds, rain squeezes down in great sheets.

Northern India and parts of eastern Malaysia get heavy rain from June through September from the southwest monsoon. The southernmost parts of India, Sri Lanka, and most of Southeast Asia get their rain from the northeast monsoon, between November and January. Monsoon rains are strongest and most powerful in India and nearby countries and in Southeast Asia. Weaker monsoons, however, do occur in other parts of the world, including Mexico and the southwestern United States.

In India, the monsoon rain helps food crops grow. But the rain also grows art, music, and stories. Old paintings show kings and queens, gods and people watching the sky, waiting for rain. For hundreds of years, composers have written music inspired by the season. One musical *raga*, or "scale," called "Megh Malhaar," is supposed to help bring rain. Classical Indian dances have special hand gestures for rain, others for storms, still others for lightning.

The rains can also be frightening and dangerous. In some places, they come with such force that floods result. Fields and houses are swept away, and sometimes thousands of people are left homeless. Traffic is forced to a halt for days in cities and towns. Businesses have to close. But if the rains don't come at all, the crops will die and there will be no rice, no wheat—no food! And so the monsoon is both loved and feared.

Monsoon Activities

Science Curriculum Standards

Explore Monsoons

After locating India on a globe, explore monsoons with your students in order to learn more about this South Asia weather phenomenon. Begin at the PBS Nature Web site at www.pbs.org/wnet/nature/monsoon/html/.

Pair the sharing of information from this Web site with a reading of *Flood and Monsoon Alert!* by Rachel Eagen (Crabtree Publishing, 2005). Invite students to discuss monsoon weather patterns, monsoon predictions, monsoon preparedness, and the effects of monsoons on animals.

> #### Science Standards
>
> #### Earth and Space Standards
> - Understands atmospheric processes and the water cycle
>
> #### English Language Arts Standards
>
> #### Writing Standards
> - Gathers and uses information for research purposes
>
> #### Reading Standards
> - Uses reading skills and strategies to understand and interpret a variety of informational texts

Watch Out! Weather

The main character in *Monsoon* lives in India where there are long dry seasons followed by rainy seasons as Uma Krishnaswami explains in her author's note "About the Monsoon" on pp. 115. Both types of weather—hot, dry weather and dramatic rainy weather that sometimes causes dangerous floods—define the climate of South Asia.

Ask students to think about the weather that defines their region of the world. What are the normal weather patterns? What dramatic weather events occur where they live? Are any of them dangerous? Do they know how to handle that danger?

Invite kids to learn about weather preparedness for your region. You might like to use the following Owlie Skywarn's weather booklets from the NOOA with them:

- *Watch Out ... Hurricanes Ahead!* www.nws.noaa.gov/om/brochures/owlie-hurricane.pdf

- *Watch Out ... Lightning Ahead!* www.nws.noaa.gov/om/brochures/owlie-lightning.pdf

- *Watch Out ... Tornadoes Ahead!* www.nws.noaa.gov/om/brochures/owlie-tornado.pdf

- *Watch Out ... Floods Ahead!* www.nws.noaa.gov/om/brochures/owlie-floods.pdf

- *Watch Out ... Winter Storms Ahead!* www.nws.noaa.gov/om/brochures/owlie-winter.pdf

- *Watch Out ... Storms Ahead!* www.nws.noaa.gov/om/brochures/OwlieSkywarnBrochure.pdf (includes hurricanes, lightning, tornadoes, floods, and winter storms)

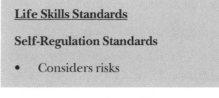

Science Standards

Earth and Space Standards

- Understands atmospheric processes and the water cycle

Life Skills Standards

Self-Regulation Standards

- Considers risks

Prepare for Weather Posters

Once students have learned about the best ways to be prepared for severe weather, invite them to make a series of posters for the most likely types of severe weather in your region. Ask them to be sure to include a definition of the weather type, three facts about dangers from the weather event, and three ways to prepare for the weather. Instruct students to use the Prepare for Weather Posters planner on p. 119 to gather and record their information before they begin.

Science Standards

Earth and Space Standards

- Understands atmospheric processes and the water cycle

Language Arts Standards

Writing Standards

- Gathers and uses information for research purposes

Reading Standards

- Uses reading skills and strategies to understand and interpret a variety of informational texts

Life Skills Standards

Self-Regulation Standards

- Considers risks

Language Arts Curriculum Standards

Writing from the Senses

Author Uma Krishnaswami uses the senses, especially sight, sound, and smell, to bring the reader inside the story to experience the time before and during the rain. Ask students to search the story for examples of each use of the senses and list them on the Writing from the Senses chart on p. 120.

Now invite students to choose an event from their lives to write about, perhaps a time they were waiting for something. What did they see, hear, smell, taste, and touch? Again, ask them to list these things on the Writing from the Senses chart. Once they have done this, instruct them to turn to paper and use the sensory details to create a poem or brief story about the event.

Language Arts Standards

Reading Standards

- Uses reading skills and strategies to understand and interpret a variety of literary texts

Writing Standards

- Uses the general skills and strategies of the writing process

- Uses the stylistic and rhetorical aspects of writing

Waiting for the Rain

Share another "rainy" picture book with students, *Come On, Rain!* by Karen Hesse (Scholastic, 1999). Explore the similarities and differences between the two waiting-for-rain experiences.

Ask students how the following are alike and different in the two stories:

- the main characters
- the settings
- the language
- the use of the senses
- the relationships of the characters
- the endings

Invite students to use the Waiting for the Rain Venn diagram on p. 121 to record their answers.

Language Arts Standards

Reading Standards

- Uses reading skills and strategies to understand and interpret a variety of literary texts

Life Skills Standards

Thinking and Reasoning Standards

- Effectively uses mental processes that are based on identifying similarities and differences

---

Music Curriculum Connections

"Megh Malhar"

In her author's note, "About the Monsoon" on pp. 115, Uma Krishnaswami explains that "one musical raga, or 'scale,' called 'Megh Malhar,' is supposed to help bring rain." Invite students to listen to a 'Megh Malhar' with you by accessing it at <u>www. podcastdirectory.com/podshows/719135.</u>

Arts Standards

Music Standards

- Understands the relationship between music and history and culture

---

Prepare for Weather Posters Planner

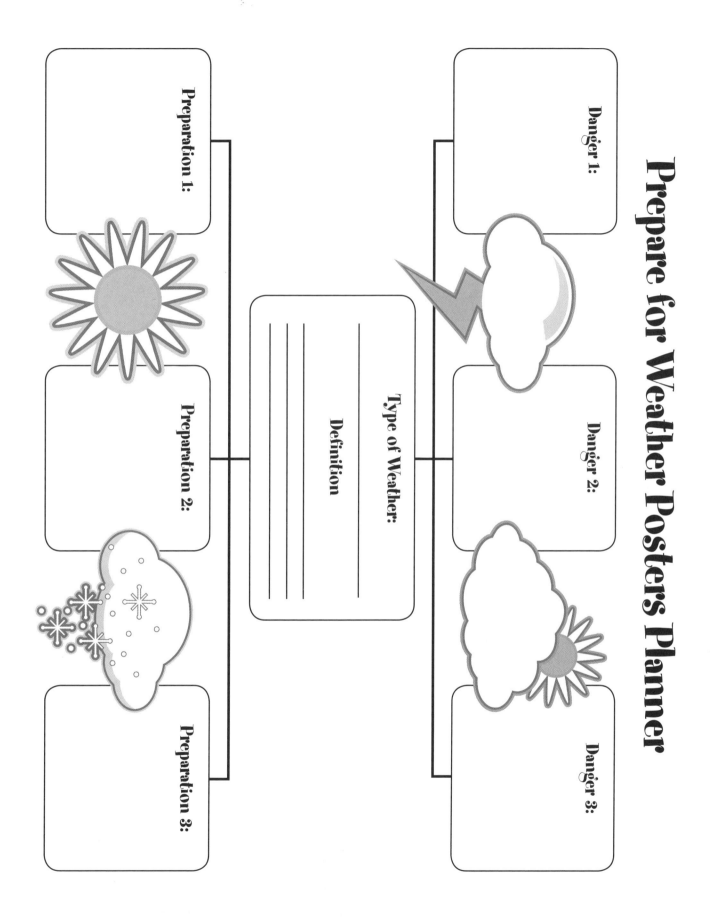

Preparation 1:

Preparation 2:

Preparation 3:

Type of Weather:

Definition

Danger 1:

Danger 2:

Danger 3:

Writing from the Senses

Sight	Sound	Smell	Taste	Touch

Waiting for the Rain Venn Diagram

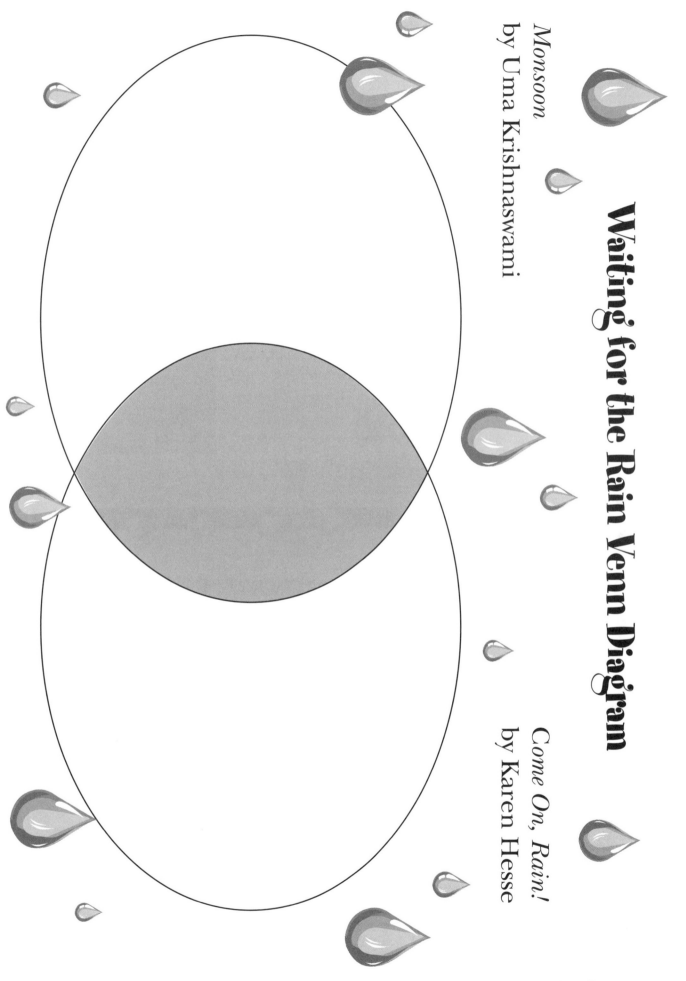

Monsoon
by Uma Krishnaswami

Come On, Rain!
by Karen Hesse

My Brothers' Flying Machine

Read *My Brothers' Flying Machine* and the interview with Jane Yolen to familiarize yourself with the book and the author. Read the book aloud to children first, so that they can enjoy the illustrations and become familiar with the story. Then, hand out a set of photocopied scripts to ten children. Katharine should be an especially skilled reader. There's a bonus one-line part (Printer) for a student who'd like to participate but not have to read much. Ask the remaining children to be the audience. Give readers time to practice their reading until they are fluent. Have performers face the audience and simply read their parts on the first run-through. Once all readers are comfortable reading before an audience, have a second reading with the opportunity to use costumes or props if desired, and to act out the story while reading.

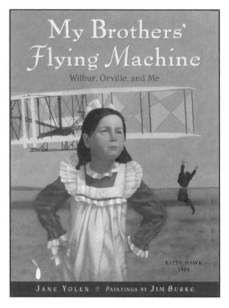

Meet Jane Yolen

Jane Yolen, often called "the Hans Christian Andersen of America," is the author of almost 300 books, including *Owl Moon, The Devil's Arithmetic,* and *How Do Dinosaurs Say Goodnight.* The books range from rhymed picture books and baby board books, through middle grade fiction, poetry collections, nonfiction, and up to novels and story collections for young adults and adults.

Her books and stories have won an assortment of awards—two Nebulas, a World Fantasy Award, a Caldecott, the Golden Kite Award, three Mythopoeic awards, two Christopher Medals, a nomination for the National Book Award, and the Jewish Book Award, among others. She is also the winner (for body of work) of the Kerlan Award and the Catholic Library's Regina Medal. Five colleges and universities have given her honorary doctorates.

Have you had a longtime curiosity for or admiration of the Wright Brothers themselves? If so, what drew you to their story? If not, did the excitement of the centennial inspire some of your interest in them?

JY: I have always been leery of flying, though I do it all the time, and the absolute fearlessness of the early pilots has always stunned me. But I wrote this book because of the centennial. And I only said I would do it when I discovered Katharine. Because so many books about the Wright Brothers have been done before, I didn't want to do one unless it could be unusual. Surprisingly, no one had ever done a picture book with Katharine at the center, as she was in their lives.

Did you first encounter Katharine Wright in the research for this book or had you known of her beforehand? How did you decide to take this unique approach to telling Orville and Wilbur's story?

JY: I was asked to do a book about the Wright Brothers and I said, "Give me a couple of days to do some reading before I tell you if I can get a handle on it." And there she was, right as I began my research. I was stunned and sure that many writers before me had written about her. But I was wrong. And when I found that out, I knew I could go ahead with the book.

In what ways did telling the story from Katharine's perspective limit or expand your telling of the story that is usually told?

JY: Well, she wasn't actually at Kitty Hawk and didn't do the inventing. But she was the brothers' sounding board when they were first working on their models. And when they went off on their flying trials, they wrote letters home, and sent that famous telegram to Katharine and their father. So she had an interesting perspective on how things were going. I liked that.

In what ways was Katharine Wright like you as a child? What was your birth family configuration? Were you—or are you—a steadfast supporter of those you love and a believer in the impossible?

JY: I am the oldest of two, but my brother was the Golden Boy in my father's eyes, so there is a bit of similarity. And I have been a supporter of his work (he's been a brilliant journalist in South America and is now a translator) all his adult life.

Please share some of the fascinating things about Katharine Wright and her brothers that you had to forego including in your story.

JY: For one thing, unlike the usual way families of the day thought about education, she was the only one of the siblings to get a higher degree, not the boys. But for me, the saddest thing was how, at the end of her life, Katharine was estranged from Orville. When in 1926 she decided to marry a man named Henry Haskell, Orville threw a fit. He raged and refused to speak to her again. Katharine and Henry got married, moved to Kansas City, and tried often to reconcile with him, but he was furious with her for leaving him when he felt he needed her to take care of him as she had all his life. But two years after the marriage, she caught pneumonia and it was clear she was going to die. Their older brother Lorin persuaded Orville to visit her, and he did, just in time before she passed away.

You write so many kinds of books. Please talk about how the writing of a picture book biography like this one is different from writing a fictional picture book. What is the appeal in the picture book biography format for you?

JY: The arc of the story the writer will tell is already there. It is real. You cannot tamper with it. But finding an interesting way into the story is the fun part.

How can readers learn more about you and your books?

JY: My Web site, and the journal on it, are there for anyone who is interested at: www.janeyolen.com.

Books by Jane Yolen

For a full list of Jane Yolen's works, visit janeyolen.com/janeworks.html.

A Note from Jane Yolen

The Wrights were a close-knit family, but closest of all were Wilbur, Orville, and Katharine. Both brothers credited Katharine with having a hand in their success. So it is fascinating to note that she did not get to fly until almost six years after that first flight.

All the incidents in this picture book have been documented in such volumes as Peter L. Jakab's *Visions of a Flying Machine: The Wright Brothers and the Process of Invention* (Smithsonian); Russell Freedman's *The Wright Brothers: How They Invented the Airplane* (Holiday House); Tom D. Crouch's *The Bishop's Boys: A Life of Wilbur and Orville Wright* (W. W. Norton); and many others.

Anything said by either of the Wright brothers or Katharine in this picture book, with the exception of "Is it a bat?" comes from letters, articles, interviews, or diary entries.

I am not alone in my admiration for Katharine. In 1981, the Gates Learjet Corporation established the Katharine Wright Memorial Award to be given annually to a woman who, behind the scenes, provides encouragement, support, and inspiration to her husband in the aeronautics industry or to a woman who has made a personal contribution to the advancement of the art, sport, and science of aviation and space flight over an extended period of time.

My Brothers' Flying Machine Script

Roles

Katharine Wright	Wilbur Wright	Orville Wright
Printer	Narrator One	Narrator Two
Narrator Three	Chorus (three readers)	

Note: Words historically spoken by Wilbur, Orville, and Katharine have been adjusted slightly for the Reader's Theater format. Consult the book for an historically accurate rendering.

Orville: When the world speaks of the Wrights, it must include our sister. Much of our effort has been inspired by her.

Katharine: I was four years old when Papa brought home a little flying machine.

Narrator One: He tossed it into the air right in front of Orv and Will.

Narrator Two: They leapt up to catch it.

Orville: Is it a bat?

Narrator Three: Or maybe it was Will who asked.

Narrator One: When at last the "bat" fell to the floor, they gathered it up like some sultan's treasure.

Narrator Two: They marveled at its paper wings.

Narrator Three: They admired the twisted rubber band that gave it power.

Katharine: I wanted to touch it, too, but they would not let me.

Orville and Wilbur:
You're too little.

Katharine: I was but three years younger than Orv, to the very day.

Narrator One: When the "bat" broke, Orv and Will fixed it together.

Narrator Two: Will directed Orv—with his busy hands.

Narrator Three: They tinkered 'til the toy worked better than when Papa first brought it home.

Katharine:	Our older brothers, Reuchlin and Lorin, looked down on such childish activity, but Will was not put off.
Narrator One:	He made one, and two, and three more "bats."
Narrator Two:	Each one was bigger than the last.
Narrator Three:	Orv was his constant helper.
Katharine:	I stood on tiptoe by the table, watching them work. Will shook his head.
Wilbur:	On a much larger scale, the machine fails to work so well.
Narrator One:	They were both puzzled.
Narrator Two:	They did not know the secret yet.
Narrator Three:	A machine twice as big needs eight times the power to fly.
Wilbur:	After that, I built sturdy kites, to sell to my pals in school.
Orville:	I made a printing press, with an old tombstone for a press bed, and wheels and cogs from a junkyard.
Katharine:	And he used the folding top of my old baby buggy that he had found out in the barn. My, it made me smile to see it.
Narrator One:	Papa and Mama applauded their efforts. Orv's press could print a thousand pages an hour.
Narrator Two:	A printer from the great city of Denver came to visit and climbed under and over Orv's baby-buggy press.
Narrator Three:	At last he laughed, amazed.
Printer:	Well, it works, but I certainly don't see how.
Narrator One:	Orv and Will made many messes, but Mama never complained.
Narrator Two:	She'd always been the one who gave them a hand building things when they were boys.
Katharine:	Poor Papa.
Narrator Three:	He knew God's word well enough, but not how to drive a nail.
Katharine:	When dear Mama died of tuberculosis, I took over her role: keeping the house, making the meals, and always giving the boys applause, even after I graduated from college and worked as a teacher.

Narrator One:	Will and Orv never went on in school.
Narrator Two:	They ran a print shop.
Narrator Three:	And then they ran a bicycle shop, repairing and making custom-built models they called the Van Cleve and the St. Clair.
Katharine:	Theirs was not the biggest bicycle shop in Dayton, but I like to think it was the best.
Chorus:	Will and Orv. Orv and Will.
Wilbur and Orville:	
	We worked side by side in the bicycle shop, whistling at the same time, humming the same tune.
Wilbur:	We even *thought* together.
Narrator One:	Some folks mistook them for twins, though they looked nothing alike.
Narrator Two:	Will had a hawk's face, and Orv a red mustache.
Narrator Three:	Orv was the neat one. He wore special cuffs for his sleeves and a blue-and-white-striped apron to protect his clothes.
Katharine:	But Will—land sake, he was a mess. I had to remind him when his suit needed pressing and when his socks did not match, or find him one of Orv's shirts when he was ready to go off to give a speech.
Narrator One:	The newspapers and magazines were full of stories of people trying to fly.
Chorus:	Lilienthal, Pilcher, Chanute.
Katharine:	The headlines read:
Chorus:	MEN INTO BIRDS
Katharine:	I wondered if such a thing were really possible.
Orville:	Insects, birds, and mammals fly every day at pleasure, it is reasonable to suppose that man might also fly.
Narrator Two:	Will wrote off to the Smithsonian.
Wilbur:	Please send all of your books and pamphlets on flight.
Narrator Three:	Will and Orv studied page after page. The first question they asked:

Chorus:	*How can we control the flight?*
Narrator One:	They knew that a bicycle is unstable by itself, yet it can be controlled by a rider.
Chorus:	*How much more control would an aeroplane need?*
Narrator Two:	Overhead, buzzards wheeled in the sky, constantly changing the positions of their wings to catch the flow of air.
Orville:	If birds can do it, so can men.
Katharine:	He seemed so certain, I began to believe it could be done. I began to believe it could be done by Will and Orv.
Narrator Three:	They built their first aircraft right in the bicycle shop.
Katharine:	I took over running the place, as Mama would have, so they might make their flying machine.
Narrator One:	That first aircraft's wings spanned a full five feet.
Katharine:	I measured it out myself.
Narrator Two:	The craft was of pinewood covered with fabric and sealed with shellac.
Narrator Three:	Like a kite, it was controlled by a set of cords.
Katharine:	When it was finished, Orv and I went off on a camping trip with a group of friends. While we were gone, Will did a sneak.
Narrator One:	He marched out to a nearby field and he flew the glider, watched only by some boys.
Narrator Two:	The thing suddenly swooped down on them.
Narrator Three:	The boys ate dust that day, I'll tell you.
Wilbur and Orville:	Our first aircraft was a big kite.
Katharine:	But a kite is not an aeroplane.
Narrator One:	So Will and Orv set about to build it bigger—sixteen or seventeen feet, large enough to carry a man but still open to all the elements.
Narrator Two:	Will lay face down on the lower wing, showing Katharine how he planned to fly.

Narrator Three:	She tried to imagine the wind in his face, the dirt and grass rushing to greet him like an old bore at a party.
Katharine:	*(Whisper.)* Is it safe?
Narrator One:	Will winked at Katharine and smiled.
Wilbur:	If you're looking for perfect safety, sit on the fence and watch the birds.
Katharine:	Dayton, Ohio, where we lived, was not the place to fly the aircraft.
Wilbur and Orville:	We needed somewhere with open spaces and strong, regular breezes.
Wilbur:	What about San Diego?
Orville:	What about St. James, Florida?
Wilbur:	What about the coast of South Carolina?
Orville:	Or the coast of Georgia?
Narrator Two:	At last they settled on Kitty Hawk on the outer banks, a two-hundred-mile strip of sand with the ocean at its face and North Carolina at its back.
Wilbur:	It's a safe place for practice.
Narrator Three:	Only sand and hearty breezes.
Orville:	Only sun and moon so bright I could read my watch all hours.
Katharine:	I kept the store.
Chorus:	Will and Orv kept the sky.
Narrator One:	Weeks, months went by in practice.
Katharine:	The boys sent me letters almost every day so that I might follow their every move.
Wilbur and Orville:	When we were home, Katharine was in our closest confidence.
Narrator Two:	At Kitty Hawk they flew the aircraft with a man—and without one—but always controlling the craft from the ground.

Katharine:	We had thought:
Chorus:	*Stand on the shoulders of giants and you are already high above the ground.*
Katharine:	But success did not come as quickly as we hoped.
Narrator Three:	Finally Will made a big decision.
Wilbur:	We cast the calculations of others aside.
Narrator One:	Back in Dayton they would start anew.
Narrator Two:	This time when they left Kitty Hawk for home, when they left the wind, and sand, the mosquitoes that left lumps like hen's eggs, they came home with a new idea.
Narrator Three:	Now they worked dawn to dusk, so absorbed in what they were doing, they could hardly wait for morning to come to begin again.
Wilbur:	We built a small wind tunnel out of an old starch box and used a fan to make the wind.
Orville:	Then we built a larger tunnel.
Narrator One:	They learned about lift and drag. They tried out many different kinds of wings.
Narrator Two:	In three years, almost to the day, after Will had written to the Smithsonian, they were ready for *powered* flight.
Narrator Three:	They built the *Flyer*, with a wingspan of just over forty feet.
Katharine:	Our friend Charlie Taylor made a twelve-horsepower engine for the *Flyer*, a motor both light and powerful.
Wilbur:	Gasoline was gravity-fed into the engine from a small tank just below the upper wing.
Orville:	The *Flyer* was so big—over six hundred pounds of aeroplane—it could not be assembled whole in our shop.
Narrator One:	Back to Kitty Hawk they went at the tag end of September 1903, carrying crates filled with aircraft parts.
Narrator Two:	It took weeks to put the *Flyer* together, weeks more to prepare for the flight.

Narrator Three:	Winter came blustering in early.
Katharine:	It was cold in camp, each morning the wash basin was frozen solid, so they wrote in their letters.
Narrator One:	They kept fiddling, tinkering, changing things.
Narrator Two:	Finally, on December 14, they were ready.
Narrator Three:	They flipped a coin to see who would be pilot.
Orville:	Will won, grinned, climbed into the hip cradle, and off the *Flyer* went, rattling down the sixty-foot track, then sailing fifteen feet into the air, where it stalled, crashed.
Wilbur:	But we were encouraged nonetheless.
Katharine:	The telegram they sent to Papa and me read:
Chorus:	*Rudder only injured. Success assured. Keep quiet.*
Narrator One:	On December 17, a cold and windy day, the *Flyer* repaired and ready, they decided to try again.
Narrator Two:	Hoisting a red flag to the top of a pole, they signaled the lifesaving station for witnesses.
Narrator Three:	Four men and a teenage boy appeared. The men helped them get the *Flyer* onto the starting track.
Wilbur:	Orv lay down on the lower wing, his hips in the padded cradle.
Orville:	Will shook my hand.
Wilbur:	*(Call out.)* Now you men, laugh and holler and clap and try to cheer up my brother.
Narrator One:	The motor began:
Chorus:	*Cough, cough, chug-a-chug-a-chug.*
Wilbur:	Orv released the wire that held the plane to the track. Then the plane raced forward into the strong wind and into history.
Katharine:	The boys sent a telegram home to Papa and me.
Narrator One:	After that, the world was never the same.
Narrator Two:	Many men went into the air.

Katharine:	Women, too. I was not the first woman to fly. That honor went to the wife of one of our sponsors, Mrs. Hart O. Berg, with a rope around her skirt to keep it from blowing about and showing her legs.
Wilbur:	She flew for two minutes and seven seconds, sitting stiffly upright next to me.
Narrator Three:	A Parisian dressmaker who watched the flight invented the hobble skirt, which for a short time was quite smart.
Chorus:	Such is fashion.
Katharine:	But how I laughed when I had my turn at last, flying at Pau in France on February 15, 1909.
Wilbur:	I took my seat beside her.
Orville:	I waved from the ground.
Chorus:	The plane took off into the cold blue.
Katharine:	Wind scoured my face 'til my cheeks turned bright red. Then I opened my arms wide, welcoming all the sky before me.

The End

My Brothers' Flying Machine Activities

Social Studies Curriculum Standards

Katharine and the Boys

While many books have been written about Wilbur and Orville Wright, only *My Brothers' Flying Machine* and a much longer nonfiction book entitled *The Wright Sister: Katharine Wright and Her Famous Brothers* have been written for children about their sister Katharine, who had a strong presence in her brothers' lives. Begin by reading more about Katharine Wright in the following books:

- *Wings and Rockets: The Story of Women in Air and Space* by Jeannine Atkins. Farrar, Straus and Giroux, 2003.

- *The Wright Sister: Katharine Wright and Her Famous Brothers* by Richard Maurer. Roaring Brook Press, 2003.

You may also wish to read a biography of her on the *Wright Brothers Aeroplane Company and Museum of Pioneer Aviation* site at www.first-to-fly.com/History/Just%20the%20Facts/katharine_wright.htm.

Ask students to discuss Katharine's contributions to her brothers and to the history of flight. As a group, make a list of her contributions and then ask students to defend the statement, "Katharine Wright played an essential role in the success of the Wright Brothers."

Women in Aviation

Just as Katharine Wright made important contributions to aviation history, so have many other women. Ask students to explore the lives of these women and create a time line of women in aviation, marking important events on a classroom or library timeline by completing and attaching a Women in Aviation Research Card on p. 136 to a date written on the timeline using string or yarn.

An excellent resource for identifying and researching these women can be found at the ThinkQuest Web site at library.thinkquest.org/21229/history.htm.

History Standards

Grades K–4: Topic 4—The History of Peoples of Many Cultures Around the World

- Understands major discoveries in science and technology, some of their social and economic effects, and the major scientists and inventors responsible for them

Language Arts Standards

Writing Standards

- Gathers and uses information for research purposes

Science Curriculum Standards

Paper Flyers Compete

Just as the Wright Brothers designed a series of planes in order to learn the best design for flight, invite your students to create the best-designed paper airplane.

Begin by reading "What Makes Paper Airplanes Fly" at teacher.scholastic.com/paperairplane/airplane.htm. Link to patterns for various styles at www.paperairplanes.co.uk/.

Establish a list of criteria for materials (size and weight of paper, number of paper clips, inches of tape, amount of glue, etc.). Next, determine the goal. Should planes be designed to fly the farthest distance or stay in the air the greatest length of time? Finally, set a date for a paper airplane competition.

Science Standards

Physical Sciences Standards

- Understands forces and motion

Nature of Science Standards

- Understands the nature of scientific inquiry

Life Skills Standards

Thinking and Reasoning Standards

- Understands and applies basic principles of hypothesis testing and scientific inquiry

Language Arts Standards
You Were There—In Words!

Invite students to read more about the flight of the Wright Brothers in the Flyer in 1903. In particular, they will find the following books interesting:

- *First to Fly: How Wilbur & Orville Wright Invented the Airplane* by Peter Busby. Crown Publishers, 2002.

- *To Fly: The Story of the Wright Brothers* by Wendie Old. Clarion Books, 2002.

Once they have a broader knowledge of the events, invite them to write a newspaper article as though they had been present at one of the attempted flights at Kitty Hawk or the final successful flight. Review the Tips for Writing a Newspaper Article on p. 137 with them before they begin.

Language Arts Standards

Writing Standards

- Uses the general skills and strategies of the writing process

- Uses the stylistic and rhetorical aspects of writing

You Were There—In Pictures!

In addition to articles, another way that journalists convey information is by writing strong or clever captions for photographs followed by "cutlines" that provide a little more information. We are lucky that Orville and Wilbur often took photographs and that their negatives have survived. You will find many Wright Brothers photographs at these two Web sites:

- memory.loc.gov/ammem/index.html (Type "Wright, Orville, 1871 1948" into the search box.)

- www.wright-brothers.org/Information/Homework/wright_photos.htm

Invite students to go to these collections of photographs, select a set that they like, and create interesting captions and cutlines for each using the You Were There in Pictures graphic organizer on p. 138.

Remind them that for each photo caption and set of cutlines, they should aim to answer the following five questions using the six question words:

- **Who** is in the photo from left to right?

- **What** is happening?

- **When** and **where** did the event/action take place?

- **Why** do the people or place look this way?

- **How** did this event happen?

Diary of a Flyer

Sometimes the best way to know and understand an historical figure is to imagine that you are walking in his or her shoes. This is what author Jane Yolen did when she wrote the story of Katharine Wright in first person. Begin by sharing several books about the Wright Brothers. In particular, the following book, which portrays the two brothers as individuals, will be useful:

- *Touching the Sky: The Flying Adventures of Wilbur and Orville Wright* by Louise Borden and Trush Marx. Margaret K. McElderry Books, 2003.

Then, invite students to write a diary or journal in the voice of Orville or Wilbur Wright. It will be helpful for them to refer to the American Memory site for an excellent timeline of the inventor's lives at memory.loc.gov/ammem/wrighthtml/wrighttime.html.

Women in Aviation Research Card

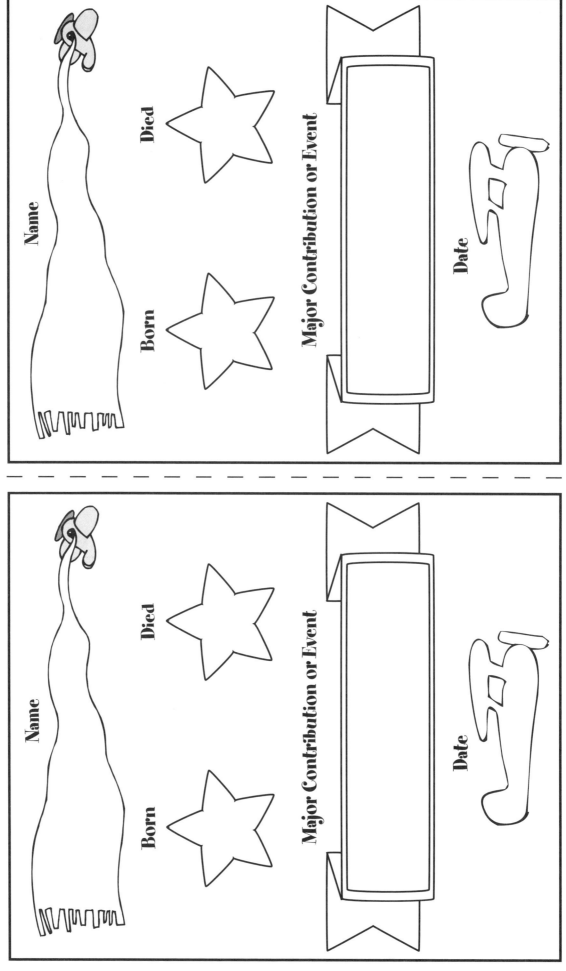

Name

Died

Born

Major Contribution or Event

Date

Name

Died

Born

Major Contribution or Event

Date

Tips for Writing a Newspaper Article

First Paragraph

Begin with a question or an interesting or surprising sentence.

Tell who, what, when, where, and why in your first sentence.

Write the most interesting information first.

Middle Paragraphs

Load up with details.

Quote from people you interviewed.

Avoid your own opinion.

Last Paragraph

End with a punchy line or a question.

You Were There–In Pictures

Oliver's Must-Do List

Read *Oliver's Must-Do List* and the interview with Susan Taylor Brown to familiarize yourself with the book and the author. Read the book aloud to children first, so that they can enjoy the illustrations and become familiar with the story. Then, hand out a set of photocopied scripts to eight children. [Note that the chorus lines are brief, so they are perfect for challenged readers who need to gain confidence with oral reading.] Ask the remaining children to be the audience. Give readers time to practice their reading until they are fluent. Have performers face the audience and simply read their parts on the first run-through. Once all readers are comfortable with their parts, have a second reading with the opportunity to use costumes or props if desired, and to use gestures or mime while reading.

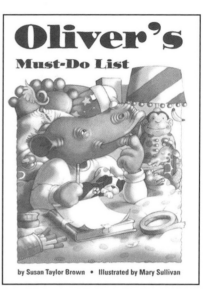

by Susan Taylor Brown • Illustrated by Mary Sullivan

Meet Susan Taylor Brown

In addition to *Oliver's Must-Do List*, Susan is the author of the nonfiction book *Robert Smalls Sails to Freedom*, the picture book *Can I Pray With My Eyes Open?* and the middle grade verse novel *Hugging the Rock*. She has served on the faculty for the Highlights Foundation Chautauqua Conference and was the yearlong Writer-in-Residence for San Jose Community School. She is also a former newspaper columnist for the *New Orleans Times Picayune* and past instructor for the Institute of Children's Literature. She lives in San Jose, California, with her husband, Erik Giberson, her dog, and over 5,000 books.

Where did the character of Oliver come from? He's a pretty long-suffering kid with an awfully busy mom. Did you draw on your experiences as a child, as a parent, or something else entirely?

STB: I wanted to write a Mother's Day book but it never came together for me. That led to brainstorming about my own childhood and about when my kids were little. My mom was a single parent who worked all day. When she came home I wanted

to play but she had chores and was always exhausted from the long work day. When my kids were little I was a stay-at-home mom but I was also trying to launch a writing career. I had to juggle work, chores, and playing-with-my-kids time. Oliver is a meshing of all of that.

I am curious about the games and activities that Oliver plays, first by himself and then with his mother. Were these favorites of yours as a child or perhaps of your own children? How did you decide what would go on Oliver's Must-Do List?

STB: Again, it is a mix of my childhood and watching my own kids play. When I was little, my mom and I wished on the first star every night and as an only child I spent a lot of time alone so I was good at the imagining part of things like making race cars out of furniture and fantasizing battles with pirates. My own children were spectacular fort builders. They were also the ones who figured out how to slide down our stairs on pillows, making our house one of the more popular ones on the block. But the peanut butter and pickle sandwiches, those are all mine. They were a childhood favorite and continue to be a comfort food to this day—thick slices of sweet pickles, creamy peanut butter, and really soft white bread. Yum, yum.

For the most part, authors don't write children's books to "teach young readers a lesson." Yet I can imagine that there might be a lesson or two readers could draw from this book. Is it possible that there's a lesson here for both adults and children?

STB: I like to think we can learn something from everything we read. I wanted to give readers a glimpse of how much fun a par-

ent and a child can have just doing simple things together. Some parents might feel a twinge of guilt midway through the story but by the end I hope they realize that it is never too late to take time to play with their children. I also hope that young readers will be empowered by the idea that Oliver spoke up for what he wanted from his mother and found a peaceful way to get it.

Readers who have read your earlier picture book, *Can I Pray with my Eyes Open?* will notice that the two books are very different in style, structure, and theme. Will you discuss the differences in the experience of writing two such dissimilar picture books?

STB: *Can I Pray with my Eyes Open?* is a spiritual book written in rhyme and based on a childhood experience that simmered in me for many years. I never thought about writing a book on prayer until an event in my adult life triggered that experience again. I also never stopped to think "will I write in rhyme or not?" The first stanza came to me in rhyme and I just followed the words for the rest of the story. I wrote it fast, a first draft in a couple of hours, propelled, I'm sure, by it having simmered for over 25 years.

With *Oliver,* on the other hand, I had many disjointed images in my head of a parent and child playing together but no story to connect them and no clear structure. I tried rhyme. I tried alliteration. I tried adding siblings and imaginary friends. It took several years of writing and revising before I found my way into the actual story.

You have also published an historical nonfiction book and most recently your first middle grade novel in verse. What calls you to write in a variety of formats and genres?

What is most fun and the most challenging about writing picture books?

STB: I'm fascinated by characters (whether fictional or based on real people) and the questions they have. When a character starts to talk to me I just want to follow him or her around and hear all about the life he or she is living. At that point I'm not really thinking about the format, I'm just interested in the story. Later I think the story waiting to be told dictates the format.

One of the most challenging things for me about writing picture books is thinking short. I love all the little details about a character but I don't have room in a picture book to share them all. I have to think powerful and compact. As for the fun stuff, I'm usually a very serious person and what I love about writing picture books like *Oliver's Must-Do List* is getting the chance to be silly. I can give myself permission to be silly when I am playing with a picture book a lot more easily than I can with a novel.

On your Web site, I see that Oliver actually takes trips around the country to schools. Tell us a bit more about Oliver and his adventures and how schools can get involved.

STB: I know many schools would like to have an author visit but can't afford the expense. And I enjoy visiting schools but have a limited amount of time to travel. So I had a stuffed Oliver made that could travel in my place. He comes in a yellow backpack with his dog, his book of knock-knock jokes, a quilt and even a peanut butter and pickle sandwich. I include a copy of the teaching guide and some reproducible activities. All of this is free to schools upon request. The only cost is mailing Oliver home. After a visit, Oliver posts about his adventures on his blog. Schools can read more and request Oliver to come visit by going to: www.susantaylorbrown.com/travel.html

How can readers learn more about you and your books?

STB: Please visit my Web site www.susantaylorbrown.com and my blog susanwrites.livejournal.com.

Books by Susan Taylor Brown

Can I Pray with My Eyes Open? Hyperion, 1999.

Hugging the Rock. Ten Speed Press, 2006.

Oliver's Must-Do List. Boyds Mills Press, 2005.

Robert Smalls Sails to Freedom. Lerner Publishing Group, 2006.

Oliver's Must-Do List Script

Oliver: Good Morning. Will you play with me today?

Mother: Let me check today's Must-Do list.

Narrator One: Oliver's mother had a list of all the things she needed to do.

Chorus: Breakfast dishes

Laundry

Ironing

Grocery Store

Clean bathroom

Vacuum

Dust

Narrator Two: She kept the list on the refrigerator. Some days it was a very long list.

Chorus: Trash

Clean closets

More laundry

Wash dog

Narrator Three: She gave Oliver a hug.

Mother: Oh, Oliver, I wish I could play, but not now. First I have to wash the breakfast dishes. Then it will be time for laundry.

Narrator One: She squirted dish soap into the sink, and little bubbles floated into the air.

Chorus:	Pop pop pop.
Narrator Two:	Oliver practiced his knock-knock jokes in front of his bedroom mirror.
Oliver:	Knock knock.
Narrator Three:	But it wasn't the same without someone to say:
Chorus:	Who's there?
Narrator One:	He took a kitchen chair and laid it on the floor.
Narrator Two:	He pretended it was a racecar, and zoomed around the room.
Chorus:	Rrrrrrrrrrrrr zoom!
Narrator Three:	But it wasn't much fun without someone to race against.
Oliver:	I guess I'll watch you fold the laundry.
Narrator One:	He grabbed his favorite red shirt and held it up to his nose to smell the clean.
Oliver:	Will you play with me now?
Narrator Two:	Oliver's mother checked her Must-Do list, then blew him a kiss.
Chorus:	Smoooooch.
Mother:	Oh Oliver, I wish I could play, but not now. I have to do the ironing. Then it will be time to go to the grocery store.
Narrator Three:	Oliver pulled all the cushions off the couch and tried to build a fort, but the walls kept falling down.
Oliver:	It's just no fun having an adventure without someone to share it with.
Narrator One:	After they went to the grocery store, Oliver helped his mother put away the groceries.
Oliver:	What about NOW? Will you play with me now?
Mother:	Goodness no! Why just look at this list. So much work still to do. Clean the bathroom. Vacuum. Dust. Mop the floors. Then it will be time for dinner.
Narrator Two:	Later, Oliver put on his pajamas and brushed his teeth.

Narrator Three:	His mother came in to say goodnight.
Oliver:	*(Whisper.)* What about now?
Mother:	*(Yawn.)* Oh Oliver, I'm sorry. Maybe tomorrow.
Narrator One:	She tucked him into bed and turned out the light.
Narrator Two:	After she left, Oliver got out of bed and stared out the window.
Narrator Three:	He tried to count the stars and find the Big Dipper, but he wasn't sure where to look.
Narrator One:	The next morning, Oliver got up very early. He made his own Must-Do list and put it on the refrigerator.
Narrator Two:	He made sure his list covered his mother's list completely.
Narrator Three:	He waited for his mother to come into the kitchen. Oliver's mother read the list.
Chorus:	Tell a joke. Drive a racecar. Build a fort. Count the stars and find the Big Dipper.
Narrator One:	Mother sighed.
Narrator Two:	She put her hands on her hips and started to whistle. She tapped her foot.
Narrator Three:	Oliver waited. And waited and waited and waited …
Mother:	Knock knock.
Oliver:	Who's there?
Mother:	Wooden shoe.
Oliver:	Wooden shoe who?
Mother:	Wooden shoe like to play with me today?
Oliver:	*(Laugh.)* You told a joke.
Mother:	*(Wink.)* Well, it IS on the list.
Oliver:	I don't suppose that you know how to drive a racecar, do you?
Mother:	Not only that, I know the perfect racetrack. Follow me.

Narrator One:	Oliver's mother grabbed the pillows off the bed and showed Oliver how to race down the stairs on his stomach over and over again until they collapsed in a heap at the bottom of the stairs.
Narrator Two:	Oliver won almost every time.
Narrator Three:	She tickled him and they both giggled so hard they got the hiccups.
Oliver:	Do you know how to build a fort?
Mother:	I'll have you know I am a champion fort builder.
Narrator One:	Oliver's mother pulled out the card table and draped a big blanket over the top.
Narrator Two:	She took all the kitchen chairs and made a big wall around the fort.
Narrator Three:	Inside the fort they ate peanut butter and pickle sandwiches and played cards and sang silly songs.
Mother:	Shush. Do you hear that? I think pirates are trying to attack the fort.
Chorus:	Argh! Shiver me timbers.
Narrator One:	Oliver grabbed his imaginary sword.
Oliver:	*(Shout.)* I'll save you.
Mother:	*(Yell.)* Take that and that!
Narrator Two:	Together they battled pirates.
Chorus:	Argh!
Oliver:	*(Cry.)* They got me.
Narrator Three:	He stumbled out of the fort, clutching his hand to his chest. He spun around in a circle three times and collapsed onto the floor.
Mother:	My hero!
Narrator One:	She kissed him in the forehead.
Narrator Two:	After dinner Oliver had a bath and put on his pajamas.
Oliver:	Guess it's time for bed, huh?
Mother:	Not yet. There's still one thing left on our list.

Narrator Three:	She took some pillows and a big quilt outside to their backyard.
Narrator One:	Together they counted the stars and listened to the crickets sing.
Chorus:	Chirrup! Chirrup! Chirrup!
Narrator Two:	They even found the Big Dipper.
Oliver:	Knock knock.
Mother:	Who's there?
Oliver:	Hank.
Mother:	Hank who?
Oliver:	Hank you for playing with me today.
Narrator Three:	Oliver's mother smiled and snuggled close.
Mother:	Hank you—for making such a good list.

The End

Oliver's Must-Do List Activities

Language Arts Curriculum Standards

What Parents Must Do

Every child has had the experience of waiting, and waiting, and waiting for an adult to be done with jobs, chores, or responsibilities so they can play with them. Begin by asking students to brainstorm the reasons their parents or significant adults offer for being unable to play. List the ideas as they are suggested, in no particular order, but then extend the activity by categorizing the activities.

Begin by explaining that categorizing (or classifying) a group of things is a way of organizing it. If the class hasn't categorized before, begin by putting a pile of coins on the table and asking students to name all of the ways they could be divided into categories (color, denomination, metal, size, year minted, etc.).

Now, invite students to look at the list of reasons their parents can't play. What are the things on their must-do lists? Ask students, in small groups, to devise a classification scheme for the things listed, using the What Parents Must Do graphic organizer on p. 150. When this work is complete, invite groups to share their classifications with the class.

> **Language Arts Standards**
>
> **Listening and Speaking Standards**
>
> - Uses listening and speaking strategies for different purposes

> **Life Skills Standards**
>
> **Thinking and Reasoning Standards**
>
> - Effectively uses mental processes that are based on identifying similarities and differences

Your Must-Do List

When Oliver makes his must-do list, it is very different from his mother's. His list isn't full of tasks and chores. His list is full of fun and imagining. Invite your students to create their own must-do lists. If they had a perfect day to spend with an adult they love (a parent, a grandparent, an aunt or uncle, or another special adult) what would each of them include on the Must-Do list?

Ask each student to fill out the Your Must-Do List graphic organizer on p. 151. Once their lists are complete, invite each student to write a letter to his or her special adult, inviting that person to spend a day doing many of the things on the Must-Do list. Attach the list and help each student to mail the letter to his or her special adult.

> **Language Arts Standards**
>
> **Writing Standards**
>
> - Uses the general skills and strategies of the writing process
> - Uses the stylistic and rhetorical aspects of writing

Knock-knock. Who's There?

Oliver loves knock-knock jokes. Many of your students probably do, too. Invite students to design their own knock-knock jokes in the classroom.

A good place to start is by reading many knock-knock jokes in order to discover "Who's There?" responses that work. Of course, in addition to borrowing successful responses to the question in order to build the joke, you'll encourage kids to come up with original ideas, too.

Begin with these books:

- *Back-to-School Belly Busters: And Other Side-Splitting Knock-Knock Jokes That Are Too Cool for School* by Katy Hall and Lisa Eisenberg. HarperFestival, 2002.

- *Knock-knock Jokes* by Pam Rosenberg. Child's World, 2004.

- *Ridiculous Knock-knocks* by Chris Tait. Sterling, 2001.

You might also enjoy this Web site, www.azkidsnet.com/JSknockjoke.htm. (**Note:** Because it is privately operated, you may want to be sure to examine the content periodically.)

Invite kids to create their own knock-knocks. jokes.

Language Arts Standards

Reading Standards

- Uses reading skills and strategies to understand and interpret a variety of literary texts

Writing Standards

- Uses the stylistic and rhetorical aspects of writing

Stand-Up Comedy

Once students have created a host of knock-knocks, stage a morning or afternoon stand-up comedy event in which they have a chance to deliver their knock-knock jokes to a fresh audience, whether of parents or other classes of students.

As they prepare, emphasize the importance of proper practice and delivery of a joke in order for it to be funny. Review the tips and then post How to Tell a Knock-Knock Joke (from p. 152) in the library or classroom.

Language Arts Standards

Writing Standards

- Uses the general skills and strategies of the writing process

- Uses the stylistic and rhetorical aspects of writing

Listening and Speaking Standards

- Uses listening and speaking strategies for different purposes

Life Skills Standards

Working with Others Standards

- Contributes to the overall effort of a group

Social Studies Curriculum Standards

All Kinds of Families

Oliver appears to be an only child living alone with his mother. They have a family of two. *Oliver's Must-Do List* provides a perfect opportunity to talk about the many variations of family structure among our students.